Return to the Wild

The Story of a Captive Otter and His Journey to Freedom

Danelle Murray and Brendan Murray

To our children, Spencer and Rebecca, who share our devotion to animals and who were as much a part of Lazarus's journey and the success story of his release as we were.

Foreword

Return to the Wild is a terrific book about a mammal that is on most people's list of Top 10 favourite animals. Along with penguins and pandas, dolphins and meerkats, otters rank high in many countdowns of favourite species.

These charming creatures are certainly high on my list of favourites, and with my job as a wildlife TV presenter and producer, I've been lucky enough to have been filmed with 3 of the world's 13 otter species.

In Brazil, I've talked to the camera, while over my shoulder, 1.8-metre giant river otters *(Siamogale melilutra)* or river wolves, feasted on piranhas. In Monterey, California, I've kayaked with a sea otter *(Enhydra lutris)* floating on her back, with a flat stone on her chest that she used as an anvil to smash open shellfish! On the Shetland islands in Scotland, I've been filmed with Eurasian otters *(Lutra lutra)* hunting for crabs just metres away from me.

Otters are not just a passion on film shoots. I go out of my way to catch up with them whenever I can. In Singapore, Asian small-clawed otters *(Aonyx cinereus)* have become city slickers and I've watched a group of 10 waiting for a gap in the traffic to cross a busy road. From a hide In Wilderness, South Africa, I was entranced as a malachite kingfisher looked down from its perch on a family of Cape clawless otters *(Aonyx capensis)* playing in the shallows.

These African animals, the third largest otters in the world, are the same species as Lazarus, the star of this absorbing book. I was fascinated by how Brendan and Danelle Murray went about returning an otter to the wild. The Murrays, from the Owl Rescue Centre in South Africa, share the trials and tribulations, as well as happy and euphoric moments during this fiendishly complicated process.

Rescuing and rehabilitating over 1,000 owls a year has given the Murrays plenty of experience preparing animals for life in the wild, but a hand-reared cape clawless otter was a whole new challenge. At the start of their journey together, Lazarus was even afraid of water.

The book also has some fascinating human characters, and the relationship between animals and people is a constant theme. The authors make some remarkable observations of animal intelligence and the cleverness of Lazarus, the otter, but the book features a smart baboon that could be depended upon to change the signals on railway tracks.

The book is dedicated to the Murray's children, Spencer and Rebecca, because the Lazarus project was a family affair. Some of the most heart-warming passages in the book involve the children, who are as passionate and dedicated to returning animals to the wild as their parents are.

I won't give away whether the family succeeded in giving Lazarus, their beloved otter, independence in the wild. You will have to read this marvellous book to find out what happened.

Nigel Marven
Wildlife Television Presenter and Producer

Realising that there is a rapid decline in owls' numbers and that they have become one of the most common wildlife casualties in veterinary practices, Brendan and I decided about twelve years ago to focus all our efforts on conserving them. We founded the organization, Owl Rescue Centre, and created a sanctuary for owls in the rural area of Hartbeespoort in the North West Province of South Africa. Our objective was to put projects in place that would protect owl species and reduce their mortality rate. Our work has since expanded to help other vulnerable species and we take in well over a thousand owls every year through our rescue efforts. The owls and other wildlife are rehabilitated and when they can survive on their own in the wild, are released in the Owl Sanctuary, a farm located within a 12,000-hectare protected conservancy, or on one of our partner wildlife reserves.

Owl Rescue Centre is a registered nonprofit company and a permitted rehabilitation facility that is dedicated to the protection of owls and wildlife in South Africa. Our efforts are aimed to decrease the risk factors to the owl species' population, accomplished through rescue and rehabilitation, education, habitat preservation, and awareness. Superstition is a big cause for the persecution of owls in South Africa, and we work hard to create awareness among communities to help them understand that owls share our natural habitat and play an important role in the ecological system by keeping the rodent population under control. Our education is aimed at providing insight into the misperceptions people have about owls and to inform them that owls pose no threat to human beings.

Our work is more than just a job for us, it is a way of life. We are fully invested in what we do, and our passion for the natural world extends to our kids, Rebecca and Spencer, who are often involved in our work.

Owl Rescue Centre

www.owlrescuecentre.org.za

IUCN

SSC
Species Survival Commission

Otter Specialist Group

Contents

Preface

This is a story so unique that it deserves only to be told in the most genuine reconstruction of the memories of the two people who experienced it first-hand. Because we wanted to preserve the authenticity of our personal experiences with Lazarus, my husband Brendan and I decided to co-author this book. Even though we shared these encounters and worked on the release project together, two people can never experience something in completely the same way. Our experience of the world around us is made up of not only external stimuli but also by how we interpret these specific events and what they mean to us at that particular time in our life. This story is therefore told through each of our own individual reflections on returning a captive otter back to the wild.

Writing a book together has its challenges, and we encountered a few problems as we began working on the manuscript together. We have two completely different writing styles and often conflicting opinions on storytelling techniques were at play—two minds with differing viewpoints and narration angles. To overcome this without overshadowing either account or forcing one to conform, the book was divided to give voice to each author's own version of events. The main story is told through my authorship, but in small parts of the book the first-person account swap from mine to Brendan's.

Brendan wrote short accounts detailing his own profound experiences of working with Lazarus, which add depth to the story and expands on it. Brendan's accounts are placed between chapters to make it easy for you, the reader, to keep track of who is telling the story. We hope that through this, you get to know us, share in our fondest memories of Lazzy, and partake in each of our individual experiences, but also get a fuller and more detailed depiction of Lazarus's passage to freedom. It is one story written from two perspectives.

The original idea of a book about Lazarus was to put a photo journal together of all the events during his release process. After some consideration, we realised that we had far too much to say about each of those captured moments in the photographs. Mere captions would not do a story of this kind justice. In working with Lazarus, we gained so much knowledge, perspective, and insight into the Cape clawless otter (*Aonyx capensis*) as a species, and came to the believe that it was our duty of sorts to write about our experience. Through this book, we hope to encourage the protection and conservation of all otter species. Achieving this would be the highest honour we could wish for.

Cape clawless otters are the second largest freshwater otter species in the world. Of all otter species, they rank as third largest, just after the giant otter (*Pteronura brasiliensis*) of the Amazon and the sea otter (*Enhydra lutris*), with a weight of between 12 kg to 18 kg. Cape clawless otters are one of two species that occur here in South Africa and are distinguished from the spotted-necked otter (*Hydrictis maculicollis*) that occur in the same areas as the Cape clawless otter mainly by their size, lighter colour, and absence of spotted markings on the neck and throat.

The most remarkable characteristic of the Cape clawless otter, as the name appropriately suggest, is the lack of claws on their "fingerlike" front and their back toes. Only a tiny nail is present on three of the hind toes, which is used for grooming. Cape clawless otters only have webbing in their back toes, another thing that sets them apart from the other otter species that have webbed front and hind toes. Although known as a river otter species, Cape clawless otters are often spotted along the coastline, frolicking in the waves on the beach and snacking on mussels off the rocks, a favourite food source of this otter.

When we first took on the task of releasing Lazarus back into the wild, we knew that we would have our work cut out for us to facilitate his learning, helping him to develop the skills he would need to survive in the wild. This turned out to be even harder than what we had imagined and presented many challenges to navigate around, but it was the reward of working with Lazarus that exceeded all of our expectations. We saw ourselves as his teachers and the facilitators of his development, but little did we know how much we would learn from him during this process.

Lazzy's story in many ways is a perfect analogy of overcoming challenges in our own lives - to have courage, persistence, confidence, and determination in what we wish to achieve. He reminded us, through his remarkable transformation, that it is never too late to be the person that we want to be and to live the life we were meant to have.

Our photos and video clips of Lazarus were widely publicized on social media and in magazines and newspapers around the world, and Lazzy gained thousands of eager fans following his brave journey.

This is his story.

Chapter 1

Meeting Lazarus

It was September, my favourite time of the year - Springtime. A time when the earth is afresh with new beginnings. The air is perfumed with a gentle scent of blossoms as the trees awaken from their winter sleep. It is a time of the year when all of your senses are aroused and Nature demands your attention. It is also the best time for an animal to start their new life in the wild.

I woke up long before my alarm clock went off. With all the excitement for the day ahead, I could not get to sleep the night before, and yet I felt refreshed, wide awake and ready to go - energised by my zeal to begin our work with an animal I simply adored. Our busy schedule leaves little time for planning, and Brendan and I rushed past each other in a frenzy that morning to get everything packed into the Land Rover. We left home while it was still dark outside. The kids, still in a daze and half-asleep, got into the car, wrapped themselves up in their duvets, and nodded off again as we departed from the Owl Sanctuary, heading off on the hour-and-a-half journey to the release farm.

When we arrived, the sun had just broken through the dark skyline with its golden glimmer glaring in the east. Baby animals peaked out from under their mom's bellies as the Land Rover rumbled past on the dusty sand roads. I opened my window to invite the crisp morning air in, fragranced with the scent of animals, earth, and sweet vegetation. The landscape at the entrance of the farm consisted of hectares and hectares of jejune grasslands and bushveld thorn trees. As we continued our journey, the scenery changed into a wonderland of tall shady evergreen trees, dense undisturbed wild vegetation, and mountains. Down by the river, leafy branches arched over the thoroughfare that ran alongside the river to form an underpass that enveloped us in greenery.

By 7:00 a.m. on that Sunday, the balmy sun was already beating down on us as we sat waiting on the riverbank. We had been up since 4:00 a.m to be in time to do our final checks of the enclosure. Our Saturday was spent digging trenches, planting poles, and pulling and fastening wires to erect the temporary enclosure where the otter would be kept safe in his new environment until such time that he would be ready to survive in the wild. There was so much to be done. It took weeks of preparation to have everything ready for Lazarus's arrival, but most of the work got crammed into the last two days.

We had hoped in our planning stages to get a sponsor on board, a company that might supply the materials for the 60 m^3 enclosure that was needed as a temporary holding pen for Lazarus to get used to his new environment. The enclosure needed to be made from strong, welded, galvanised mesh to make sure that Lazarus could not break out before he was ready - or that predators could not get in. One steel company after the other had gone belly-up in the tough economic climate, and our search for a donor was fruitless. Many companies simply said that they were in debt rescue and could not possibly contribute in any way.

Funding had been a struggle even before the recession had taken its full effect. As far as sponsorship is concerned, wildlife conservation falls to the bottom of causes to get the nod from Corporate Responsibility Investment funds: below social welfare, education, arts and culture, social groups, or even sport. Although I understand why companies support all these charitable initiatives before supporting animal conservation, I can't help but find it deeply ironic that a country so rich in wildlife pays so little attention to its preservation. Funding our work has always been an uphill climb. I have always hoped that people would come to understand our interdependence as humans on animals and nature. Maybe someday they will. I can only hope that when this realisation finally sets in, it won't be too late and that there will still be enough time left to save all living species, even the small ones that are believed to be insignificant, from extinction.

About a week before our planned meeting of Lazarus, we received a generous gift from a good friend and fellow conservationist, Georgina. She had intended the donation to be for an enclosure for the release of two black sparrow hawks that we had taken in for rehabilitation at the Sanctuary. In the end, the release of the hawks was done from a platform that we were able to construct from material we had readily available. Thus, the funds were instead allocated to the otter release.

When finally, the release enclosure stood ready, there was nothing left to do but wait. We sat anxiously with excitement on the bank of the Crocodile River, anticipating the arrival of Lazarus and Dr. Schouwstra, the regional wildlife vet who had bottle-raised Lazarus and cared for him up to now. The otter was rescued as a baby when he somehow got separated from his mother, and he was brought to the veterinary practice by a wildlife rehabber for care.

I picked up some withered, dried leaves off the sand around me, fidgeting with it between my fingers. Time seemed to be moving at a passive pace. I felt impatient, something I would have thought impossible to feel in such a tranquil environment. Perhaps it was eagerness rather than restlessness that I felt.

"Do you think she's still coming? Maybe she changed her mind," I said to Brendan.

"It's still early. She's probably held up by the road works on the way," he reassured me.

Dr. Schouwstra had agreed to entrust us to introduce Lazarus, a Cape clawless otter who had spent the first four years of his life in captivity, to the wild. She could not stand the thought of him spending his whole life in a cage but had been concerned that it was already too late to release him to fend for himself. She had tried before but failed to successfully free him. Lazzy (as he came to be known later) was in perfect health and there should be no reason why he could not pull through in the wild, other than that he had never acquired the necessary skills for survival.

The release of an otter is a complicated process and requires the right habitat, enclosure, and careful systematic integration monitoring. Dr. Schouwstra's veterinary practice did not have the necessary resources, premises, and manpower to facilitate the release process and we therefore offered our help. We had a release farm at our disposal that would provide the perfect habitat for an otter, with plenty of prey availability and safety (away from human habitat or interference), and where others of his kind have been spotted. We offered to erect the necessary structure for the "soft release" process, and have a volunteer permanently placed at the site for monitoring and feeding.

Brendan, like many of his generation, developed a strong affection for otters as a child after watching a film called *Ring of Bright Water* (1969), an adaptation of the book with the same name by Gavin Maxwell. It is about a man and his pet otter and the relationship that develops between them. Brendan could identify with the character of Graham

Merrill, the main character in the story, and a conceptual link between himself and the animal was also established. He subsequently spent his younger years searching for otters along rivers - a privilege he had over me, growing up in a time when kids could still roam free - and later studied many otters in the Okavango Delta in Botswana. Ever since I met him, an otter has always been on top of his list of favourite creatures.

I, on the other hand, had had no interactions with otters until the day I met Lazzy. I had spent many hours paddling up and down the Touws River in Wilderness, on the Garden Route of South Africa, hoping, wishing, yearning for the rare opportunity of spotting a Cape clawless otter. After years of searching, otters seemed to me much like unicorns, and I had become worried that I would never be able to fulfil my dream of coming face-to-face with an animal that represents all of life's joy. Of all the animals, it was the one I longed most to see. Otters are not only playful but considered one of the most intelligent animals on Earth. Humankind have gained much of our most valuable knowledge from the animal kingdom, and otters make a fascinating study. I was excited to finally get the opportunity to work with one.

I did what I always do when taking on a new subject; I researched every possible source of information available to me that could help me understand the nature and behaviour of such a special and intelligent animal. Brendan and I follow two rules when getting involved with a new species: we make sure we know everything we can about the animal's natural behaviour and habitat, and we do not "reinvent the wheel." We look at previously documented success with rehabilitation and release of a species and see how we can adopt and possibly improve on the information at hand. If all else fails, we turn back to nature as the voice of reason. Fortunately, Lazzy had his very own expert, his own personal vet, on standby and she would provide us with any further necessary information we might need.

Tjitske Schouwstra and her husband, Marcelle, arrived shortly after 8:00 a.m. She has a demeanour uncommon for a woman of her stature and qualifications, and our dealings with her had always been casual. She inspected the release enclosure with reasonable objectivity and was pleased with the prospect of a successful release process. Maggie, Tjitske's golden retriever who had grown up with Lazarus and had been his best friend and companion, made the trip out too. She promptly jumped from the van as Dr. Schouwstra opened the back doors, excited by the smells that come with a new environment. Lazarus was taken out of the van, and the carrier he was in placed on the ground. He was twisting and turning inside the small space. Brendan asked Spencer, our son, to take Maggie to the river for a swim while the rest of us stayed behind and Brendan and I became acquainted with Lazarus for the very first time. Maggie and Lazarus, oblivious to the situation, would finally part ways that day as the otter's long journey back to the wild was about to start.

Lazarus was even more beautiful in real life than I had imagined. No photograph would entirely capture his charm. He was quite an eyeful. His dark, chocolatey brown coat was a scruffy mess of knots but he was still as handsome as anything. Otters normally have a velvety sleek pelage, and my guess was that he lost this by not bathing himself in water often enough. We've seen owls (that we have confiscated from the illegal pet trade) that have given up preening after living in captivity for extended periods. Could Lazzy have given up on the natural process of grooming? In the wild, this is an act needed for the secretion of a thin layer of body oil from the otter's sebaceous glands, which coats the hair and is responsible for its smooth and silky appearance. The coat plays an essential role in keeping an otter warm in cold water.

Lazarus looked up at me with his beady dark eyes, which appeared soft and kind. Those gentle eyes, along with his rounded nose, disproportionately large for his face, gave him a winsome, innocent appearance that stole my heart in that very first second we met.

Lazarus was placed inside his enclosure and we watched with great amusement as he curiously explored every corner of his new temporary home. He seemed both excited and nervous. A large water trough, big enough for him to swim in, was the focal point inside the enclosure. He cautiously danced along the edge of the water pool and groaned as Dr. Schouwstra tried to give him a gentle nudge to jump in. His fingers and feet tightly gripped all along the edges, and he wore an expression of alarm. But the otter managed to stand firm without losing his balance or slipping off the boundary. This was as close as what he would venture near the foreign body of water for now. He ran inside the large wooden house that stood in the corner of the enclosure, then outside, on top of it and back inside again. He walked along the perimeter of the enclosure's fence, sticking his tiny hand through and reaching to whoever stood close. The kids giggled in delight as they watched his antics.

Brendan, Marcelle, and the vet stood back, having a conversation, while I sat mesmerized, flat on the ground next to the enclosure. The kids stood next to me and giggled in delight as they watched his antics. Brendan called me away to say goodbye to Dr. Schouwstra and Marcelle as they were about to leave, and I sheepishly joined the adult conversation.

We stayed a few more hours with Lazarus before we had to set off to attend to an owl rescue. It felt somehow strange leaving him there on his own. He must have felt a little scared and confused in this unfamiliar environment. He collected all the fish and food we left for him and stored it inside his wooden house, as if he were a survivalist stockpiling in preparation for a catastrophe. Returning several times, he would grab the food and glance over at us before tucking his hand into his body to carry the food away, hobbling along on his other three legs. One by one he took the fish we had put out to go store it. After making sure he had enough food to see him through the night - he was certainly not going to be hungry - we promised to return bright and early the next morning.

Early Impressions

By Brendan Murray

I was around eight or nine years old when I watched *Ring of Bright Water*. It was about a tame otter that was, if my memory serves me well, bought from a pet shop in London. His name was Mij. The rough story plot was that the gent who acquired Mij came to the realisation that keeping an otter in his apartment's bathtub was less than ideal, and he took the decision to move to the countryside. As an animal-crazy kid, that movie left a big impression on me (as it probably did on many others). To then have the opportunity to wild up a tame otter 40 years later in my own life was pretty surreal.

Chapter 2

An Otter Paradise

The farm we had decided on for the release was in North West Province, right on the border of Limpopo Province, located in an inland section of South Africa that borders Botswana on its Northern region. It is called Eagle's Crest and is a beautiful, lush piece of land with a 5-m or so stretch of the Crocodile River flowing through the mountainous terrain.

It was about four years before Lazarus' release, when we were on our way to Thabazimbi to rescue a pearl spotted owlet that had fallen from his nest during a storm, that Brendan pointed to farmland on our left and remarked that he believed it to be one of the most beautiful stretches of land in the country. We travel often and this was said with no uncertainty. As we crossed a bridge and the Land Rover crested the hill, the tall trees growing along the river in the valley below looked like a green snake slithering through the bush. We could catch only a glimpse of the farm, but the portion we could see was breathtakingly beautiful. We promptly decided to stop on our way back and inquire about the owner of the property.

We are always looking for appropriate release spots for the owls and other animals that make their way to us. We take great care in our release projects, and a suitable release spot is crucial in the process. The wildlife we take in are rescued mainly because of man-caused injury, whether directly or indirectly. Choosing a release site involves many considerations: poaching and persecution of particular species; the general perception about conservation in the surrounding community; fences, roads, and electric lines, and pylons and transformer boxes, to name but a few. When we do pick a release site, we make sure that the animal has the best chance of survival as far away as possible from these threats that brought them to us in the first place. The effort put into the rehabilitation of an animal, the hours of care, would all be futile if we were not mindful of where they are released.

Tyron, the owner of Eagle's Crest, a family farm named after a nesting pair of long-crested eagles that made this mountainous land their home, had his contact number printed on a sign that he had built into the stone wall at the entrance to the farm. Brendan stored the number in his phone, but about two weeks passed before he used it. He was unsure about the approach he should take to convince someone to offer up their land for conservation. This would mean allowing us full access to the property without any limitations, erecting release enclosures and structures, and placing camera traps and monitoring devices where necessary. When Brendan called Tyron, he invited us over for coffee the very next day. We were both pleasantly surprised by his openness to the idea. We have had many doors shut in our faces before, so we were no strangers to rejection. But Tyron's demeanour was welcoming, and we soon learned that he absolutely adores animals.

Tyron's house on the farm is modest for someone with his wealth. It seemed trivial and small in comparison to its staggeringly beautiful setting, but it is but one of many properties he owns spread out around the country. He has a house in the city that is well-furnished in comparison to where he stays when he visits his girlfriend in Sandton. Tyron explained how his fondness of the farm grew as he got older. Although it is a family farm, as a young man Tyron had no interest in it, nor for the rustic bush house on a farm that is about as close to paradise as one could ever hope for. He admitted that he had not always loved the farm. It was too isolated and too quiet for the liking of his younger self, but as time passed, he learned to appreciate it and stopped worrying about what he could be missing out on. He became sentimental about the farm as he aged. The farmhouse is decorated only with necessities; none of the usual ornaments and photographs found in a home are here.

The kitchen cupboards are bare and there was only a tiny bit of milk, enough for our three cups of coffee, in the fridge. Tyron seemed uncomfortable with the task of making coffee for guests. I realized that he must seldom get visitors on the farm. I offered to take over to release his tension, and made us all a cup of coffee to enjoy while we sat down on the living-room couch to discuss our needs for a release site. I felt right at home. Tyron is in his late seventies but could easily pass for someone at least twenty years younger. He spoke of his girlfriend in Johannesburg like a naughty schoolboy, with a slightly sheepish smile dancing on his face.

"She doesn't like the farm," he admitted. "She's too scared to stay here so I live here alone and visit her on weekends."

I noticed that he obsessively checked the doors to make sure that he had not forgotten to close them after we entered. One door led onto an enclosed veranda and a second into the living room.

"I don't like snakes," he said, "They'll make themselves right at home if you don't watch out and by accident leave a door open through which they could sneak in."

He then fell straight into a story about a fight he had with one of his neighbours, a farmer down the road. He was furious when he heard that the farmer had killed an African python.

"What an idiot!" he said. "I don't like snakes but there is no need to kill them. This is their home, you know. Where are they supposed to go?"

Tyron rambled on about hunters and how much he dislikes them and how he was deceived by their talk of supposedly necessary culling. He had been approached by a group of hunters who had convinced him that it was necessary to get rid of some of his stock on his farm for the purpose of conserving the habitat.

"They scared all the darn animals away! I have not seen the wildebeest or giraffes since. They have been hiding away for weeks."

Tyron is as ignorant as they come about animals, but with a heart of gold where conservation is concerned. He kept mentioning a tiger that leaves its prey hanging from trees and it took me a while to grasp what he was referring to. There are no tigers in Africa, certainly not wild ones stalking the African plains. He was, of course, referring to a leopard, which was a resident on the farm. He did not mind when the big cat took one of his antelope.

"That's just nature," he said.

Animals hunt for food for survival, unlike some humans who are motivated to hunt by pride or greed. But Tyron is dead scared of leopards. His fear of the animals who share his immediate surroundings is almost childlike, but at the same time he also has great respect for them. We had struck gold as far as a perfect release site was concerned.

Tyron asked none of the usual questions we get. We once flew to a well-known game reserve to meet with the owners of an upmarket lodge to discuss the possibility of using it as a release site. Richard, a pilot who flew rescue missions for us all over the country, offered to take us there by plane. We were picked up from the airstrip by the lodge manager in his game-viewing vehicle and upon our arrival at the lodge, an entourage of staff stood waiting, each with a two-way radio in hand, ready to lead us over a bridge to a building called the "Owners House." The place was breathtaking, like an African castle if such a thing should exist.

The owners of this game reserve were Dutch. They had just arrived back in Africa from Europe - a trip they did four times a year, every year. The place was uncomfortably fancy, and it felt like we were meeting with Victorian royalty. The pair had an air about themselves, apparent in their forced greeting, as if their time were too valuable to spend on two people who work with animals for a living. They had a pompous, haughty demeanour, which I did not like one bit. They slouched in their chairs and shot questions at us like it was a job interview and we were at the mercy of their approval.

The questions were all about their own personal interest: "What benefit is this to the lodge?" "Would our guests be able to see these owls?" "This wouldn't cost us anything, would it?" And so on and so on.

Tyron asked none of this. He spoke like he was meeting with two old friends. There was no need for any of these types of questions; he knew that he was in like-minded company and a silent agreement was formed. It was purely about the animals. He seemed to be hungry for company and we stayed for a few hours sharing stories. Then we drove around the farm looking for a spot to release eight marsh owls that were ready to be introduced back into the wild. We wanted a spot with both wide open grassland and marshy terrain, but instead decided that the farm would be better suited to release two pearl spotted owlets (*Glaucidium perlatum*) and an African scops owl (*Otus senegalensis*) I had raised out of the egg. We released the marsh owls from Mziki Nature Reserve, not far from Tyron's farm as the crow flies, where larger open fields were better suited to this species' requirements.

A week after our meeting, we camped out on Tyron's farm to observe the resident owl population of the area. The kids went to Grandma and we spent the night on a dry riverbank, sleeping in the Land Rover. When Brendan and I got married, it had not been possible for us to go on honeymoon. I would tease that he still owes me one, and over the years we ended up referring to any sleep-out occasion without the kids as our "honeymoon." As a result, we have several a year and I can no longer protest about it! These are special times, moments of bliss when I genuinely enjoy our line of work. Tyron had made a cottage available to us for use whenever we needed it, but we opted to set up camp in the Landy instead. We made a fire and cooked our supper under the stars.

We had become so attuned to the typical natures of the different owl species that the very terrain would tell us which owl we could expect to see. To prove this, we played a game in which we went for a long walk along the farm roads, in the dead silence of the night. Suddenly, I'd stop, shine the torch up into a tree, and say "There!" Between the darkness the spotlight would fall on, say, a southern white-faced owl sitting in the branches of a large thorn tree above our heads.

Over the next few months, the farm became a second home to us, and many of the owls that came into the Sanctuary were released there. We camped out many nights to observe the released owls and to monitor their progress. A few years down the line, little did we know that this would become the place where Lazarus would find his own freedom.

Building the release enclosure.

Spencer helps Brendan to carry water into the enclosure prior to Lazzy's arrival.

A view over the river where Lazzy will start his new life.

Lazzy on the first day inside his release enclosure.

Chapter 3

An Otter Afraid of Water

We arrived at the enclosure early the next morning. I had packed a flask of coffee and picnic basket with breakfast snacks. As the Land Rover came roaring along the dusty road, its engine rumbling loudly, Lazarus promptly ran to hide inside his wooden house. The sounds of a new environment, and we, who were still complete strangers to him, must have been terrifying.

When we parked the Landy on the riverbank nearby, he cautiously exited his house and came over to the gate of the enclosure to greet us. As Brendan entered the enclosure with a fresh fish for breakfast, the otter managed to squeeze past him and escape his temporary home. He ran over to where I had laid out our own breakfast spread, and sniffed and looked around curiously. You would think that I might have been terrified of this unfamiliar animal, an apex predator with a rather large set of canine teeth, but I was not. Lazarus never acted in a threatening way towards us; there is not a bad bone in his body.

We quickly realised that Lazzy was completely governed by two things: a food source and companionship. He did not run away but toward us instead. When he saw the fish Brendan had for him, he swiftly turned back and ran into his enclosure to enjoy his morning meal. Brendan and I decided that when we were sure that we'd earned his complete trust (and this was something he gave easily), we would take him for walks to the river to allow him to habituate but would only feed him inside his enclosure as an incentive to return to where he would be safe until he had gained the necessary skills to survive in the wild. We would facilitate this learning process by accompanying him to the river daily to explore and become skilled at survival in his new environment. For the next six months, we would spend approximately six hours a day with Lazarus to accomplish this.

That first morning, Lazarus gnawed greedily at the fish, gripping it tightly between his fingers, chewing on the left side of his mouth and then on the right, his large canine teeth exposed like a ravenous monster. It was his human-like fingers that captured my attention most during our first meetings. He would close his eyes at times with pure enjoyment, crunching through the bone and skin. He did not stop and ate with the same enthusiasm until the very last bit was gone.

On that first day, we also noticed something else. Something unusual. The otter explored his environment, drinking from the large trough of water inside his enclosure and curiously skirting around it, tripping like an excited toddler at a pool party but refusing to enter the water. Brendan wondered how he would behave in the river. He felt that Lazarus had been restricted from living a natural life for far too long, and limiting him for even just another day would be one day too many. We discussed letting him out now and starting his supervised exploration of the big wide world. We knew that there was a risk starting that process this early on, but we were confident that we could handle it and felt that we had managed to form a trusting relationship with this animal straight away.

We opened his enclosure and Brendan led him to the steep pathway down the embankment to the river. Lazarus was nervous at first about going to the river. He turned back a few times, and it took some convincing with food treats and coaxing to finally get him to head for the water. Lazzy's enclosure was built above the 100-year flood line in anticipation of the summer rains. The pathway leading to the river was easy for the little otter to trot on behind Brendan, followed closely by the kids, who all made it look easy, while I lagged behind trying not to slip in the slick, muddy earth and fall on my rear and land with my camera in the mud. Every day of Lazzy's journey was recorded in a video diary to use for research purposes later. This meant that we could track his progress and behavioural changes in detail, but it was difficult for me at times to keep up, with no free hand to grab for a branch should I slip.

Lazarus was as excited as a city dog in the park. He sniffed and explored, checking where we were all the time, not letting us out of his sight. No doubt he had anxiety mixed into all that excitement. He would run to each member of our family in turn, sniff, jump up, and then run along again. He did not enter the river at all that first day. He would only let a paw or his nose touch the surface of the water. We knew that the road ahead would not be an easy one, but boy, would it be worth the effort.

Conversations with Animals

By Brendan Murray

Before Lazarus arrived, Danelle and I discussed the plan of how we would go about his rehab, what we would need to do, and how much time would be needed for certain aspects. Initially, we thought he would need to stay a minimum of six weeks inside the release enclosure while he acclimatised to his new surroundings. After that we would start letting him out of his enclosure for limited periods, allowing him to explore and swim and hunt, all under our watchful eye.

Well, that was before we met the little guy. And what we planned to do and what we actually did was...not even remotely the same.

I like to talk to animals. I have long, extensive conversations with most of our rescues. I ask them how they are doing, how they got injured, if they are hungry, what they would like to eat, and other general chit-chat. Obviously, they do not answer, and I know that they do not understand a single word, but I do it anyway. With Lazzy it was no different. When he first arrived at the farm and Doc Schouwstra and her husband had left, I sat down with him and started talking.

After around the five-minute mark, I realised that I had just made a huge life decision. This was not an animal I was going to leave locked in an enclosure on a riverbank and just feed every day for the next six weeks before he could have his first minutes of freedom. No, I was going to spend all the time needed to get him back to the wild on his terms, not mine.

Lazarus had been confined to a cage his whole life so far, and I decided the very first day that Danelle and I worked with him that his real life starts right there. After we had discussed our game plan while watching him inside his enclosure munching on a fish I had brought him, I stood up from where we sat to enjoy our own breakfast, walked to the gate of the enclosure and said to him: "I'm letting you out. Please don't run away."

I opened the door, he walked out. And he did not run. And then our adventure began.

Chapter 4

A Taste of Freedom

I sat on a sandbank watching Lazzy's cheerful celebration as he got his first taste of freedom. Every now and then he would run up to me, reach up with his front finger-like paws resting on my shoulders and busily snuffle my neck with his moist nose as if to kiss me. Then he'd grunt to show his affection and appreciation and run off again. We laughed and cheered at his jolly displays. Then a sudden sadness came over me. In that moment I realised what humankind had deprived him of. His freedom was never ours to take or to give. Those who had been responsible for seeing him return to the wild before this had failed him. They failed him miserably and made a prisoner out of an innocent being.

Lazarus had been placed in the care of Dr. Schouwstra when he was still a small pup of only a few weeks old. The veterinarian was to bottle-feed him and raise him until he was old enough to go free with the promise from his rescuer, a well-known figure in the conservation world, that she would see to his release. Dr. Schouwstra had been assured that a release site had been secured. When Lazarus was about 18 months old, she contacted his rescuer again to put the release process in action. Some months later Lazarus was sent off to a farm and placed into a pre-release enclosure. He was under the supervision of a distinguished wildlife entity, but when Dr. Schouwstra went to check on his progress, she found him in poor condition. He had lost a lot of weight and looked miserable. She had no transport carrier with her at the time, and instead enticed him with a fish to jump into the back of her van, closed the doors and took him back to her practice! She agreed to return him once he was fit and healthy again.

After this incident, his would-be rescuers declined to take the otter back, telling Dr. Schouwstra that he had bitten a child while on the release farm and therefore could not return. She remained hopeful that another release site would be found. Time rolled on and fewer options for his release came up. The rehabilitation facility that had been responsible for his initial release would later state that they were concerned that, "The animal was too tame and has the potential to be dangerous."

Lazarus was just under four years old by the time he came to us and had been kept in captivity since he was a pup. The average lifespan of a Cape clawless otter is 12 years, which means that a third of his life had already been misspent in captivity. An otter is meant to spend his days alongside water, fishing and foraging for food, swimming, playing, digging burrows, finding a mate, and living a natural life. A cage offered no kind of life for an animal of his intelligence and emotional awareness. The responsibility to take him from captivity to freedom would lay heavily on our shoulders. In the months to come, Lazzy would open my mind and offer a new doorway into the psyche of an animal. While I studied psychology for many years and earned a university degree, Lazzy would teach me life lessons no textbook ever could.

If I did not already loathe the practise of keeping animals for public exhibition and exploitation, this little otter would reinforce my hatred of all such establishments and increase my aversion to people who do wrong by animals tenfold. The obsession of humans to "own" another life, that of a wild animal, is ironically also one of the biggest threats to their safeguarding. I understand that some zoological establishments are doing good work and are even a necessity for research, breeding programmes, and species-survival interventions. I just think that the lines in wildlife welfare are too easily blurred and that greed, pride, and vanity are more often the dominant forces.

Brendan and I had made a vow from the very start of our involvement in conservation: If ever our own needs take precedence over that of an animal, if ever the interests of the animal's wellbeing become vague, or if we ever find that we are exploiting our privilege of working with these beings, then we would walk away and seek another vocation. Something as small as allowing public visits to our owl enclosures for the entertainment of people and not to benefit the birds is a boundary we will not overstep. People have called us fools for this. "You can earn a lot of money through your work," they say. This may be true, but it will also cause unnecessary stress to the owls that have come to us under already stressful conditions.

Continuous human contact and exposure will mean that these owls could lose their fear of people, putting them at risk when they are released into the wild to fend for themselves. Wild animals are best protected when as little human interference as possible occurs. Of course, in some cases human intervention is necessary to put right where we have done wrong. Sometimes a bond between a wild animal and the person caring for it is essential for the rehabilitation to be successful. The importance is in understanding the difference - knowing when to get involved and to what extent - and when to keep your distance. The relationship between humans and animals is a complicated, tangled web of confusion. It has long-since caused a moral dilemma that we can only hope someday in the future will be resolved. One cannot help but be disquieted about this inherent human fallibility.

We were once asked by another rehabilitation facility we work closely with to help rescue a brown hyena. A beautiful wolf-like animal with a fascinating social structure, it had been caught in a gin trap. (The word gin is presumably short for engine, which is how the mechanical device used to trap animals was originally portrayed, as some kind of clever mechanical engine). By the time the rehabilitation community got wind of this, the female hyena had already been caught in the trap for three days. Judy Davidson from the SA Wildlife Rehabilitation Centre contacted everyone she could think of for help, and the message also came through on a mobile group we had created for wildlife emergencies. When we realised that no one closer was able to help, Brendan and I drove the 650 km to rush to the animal's rescue.

We had no information about the hyena other than that she had been spotted alive that morning. William, on whose farm the hyena was, lives in Kuruman with his family over a 100 km away. He would usually visit the farm for a few days at a time to give instructions to the farm workers and then return home to suburbia. He had asked us to pick him up from his house on our way to the hyena, so that he could direct us to the farm from there. The drive took us eight hours to reach him in Kuruman, and it was still another two-hour drive from there into the Kalahari Desert.

It was late into the night by then, and we had plenty of time to get to know William. He was in his mid-sixties and looked very much like any other farmer who had spent his life working outside under the African sun. He was a family man who put the needs of his wife and daughters above all other things. He seemed kind and generous. He brought us sandwiches, lovingly prepared by his wife and neatly packed in sandwich bags, because he knew we would not have had time to plan dinner for the road. He was a pleasant guy and we had an agreeable conversation on our way to his farm.

It was only when we turned onto the first gravel road leading to the farm that Brendan asked the question: "Did you put the gin trap out?"

"I instructed my workers to." The answer came plainly. There was a slight pause, as though he had realised for the first time that he had been responsible for the atrocity of this night. "I farm with cattle, so we place gin traps to catch jackals."

William carried on explaining that jackals come to kill the calves, and that they are cruel in their methods of hunting the young animals - as if to find a justification that might please us. He claimed that the jackals prey on the calves while the cows are giving birth to them. But nothing he could say after that would ease the sick feeling in my stomach. A whirl of disappointment, anger, and demoralised feeling filled my head.

William was raised in a culture where certain animals are seen simply as pests and a bother to the farming community. The lives of those animals have no value to these farmers, and their eradication - even with a cruel trap that causes suffering, maiming injuries, and death - is acceptable and given no further thought. They are desensitised and dissociated from feeling any empathy for the suffering of this "worthless" animal. However, when the animal turns out to be a hyena, different from their normal target, there is a sudden awakening within their conscience and help such as ours is called in to "save" the animal. In their minds, one animal's life has meaning and value while another has none. They have been conditioned over time to accept this illogical moral philosophy.

Upon our arrival, we found the female hyena dead, half buried in the sand in her struggle to free herself. The fur on her head and the tips of her ears had been singed by the scorching Kalahari sun, and had left raw red exposed skin. No water had been placed near the animal to ease her suffering; no shade to shield her from the blazing sun by those who had first found her trapped but still alive. It took three men to dig up the heavy steel bar and chain linked to the jaws of death that cost her her life. I hated my work that night. I detested the fact that my choosing to work in conservation had led me to bear witness to such cruelty. This practice continues within these communities as an "acceptable" method to manage stock loss.

Our kids faced the moral dilemma all humans battle with, between right and wrong where animals are concerned, early in their lives. I still remember the first time Spencer discovered that people eat animals.

He was four at the time. He came and stood next to me where I was preparing dinner in the kitchen. He had an inquisitive mind filled with unanswered questions. He wanted to know what different foods were made from or where they came from. He already knew that cows give us milk, chickens give us eggs, and all the normal food sources.

"But what about bread," he asked me. "Where does bread come from?"

I patiently explained how bread is made from wheat grains. Next was sugar. Another easy answer. "The sugar we use is cane sugar, which comes from a grass-type plant," I replied.

His curious mind kept going through all the options until he asked me about pork.

"Pork is meat from a pig," I said.

"What do you mean from a pig?" his eyes widening with shock and confusion.

"Pork is pig," I said more simply.

"You mean people eat animals?!" he exclaimed. It was as if his whole happy world had suddenly disappeared from under his feet. The colour drained from his face from the shock of this inconceivable notion. He had absolutely no idea.

Years later, we were working on a project in the Western Cape, walking along a secluded beach path. We were pondering over survival in deserted areas, absent of all civilisation. My son asked me whether I would ever consider hunting an animal myself if we ever got stuck somewhere without food.

"I suppose," I said, "if it means that it is the only way for us to survive." Again, I got that same look of dismay he gave me five years earlier. He seemed disappointed to hear my answer. "You eat meat," I continued.

"Yes," he answered, "but I could never kill an animal."

"But you eat meat," I said.

He responded with the same answer, this time with a bit of annoyance in his voice.

"When you eat meat bought in a supermarket, you create a demand for it. That means that people farm with animals specifically to be slaughtered for meat so you can eat it. You may not kill the animal yourself, but you allow for its killing," I explained.

Spencer looked at me with a blank expression in his eyes. He had never worked this out for himself. He had made peace with the fact that humans eat animals those five years ago and never thought about it again. The relationship between the piece of steak and the cow in a field of green pastures was broken in his mind, forgotten through conventional behaviour. It was not until this very moment that he battled this moral dilemma within himself. In the days to follow, we noticed that he pushed the meat on his plate aside. At the age of nine, he decided to be true to his convictions and beliefs, and he later announced that he had decided to become a vegetarian. He has stuck to this religiously ever since.

About a month after Spencer decided to be a vegetarian, his sister Rebecca followed suit. She simply announced: "Mommy, I love animals very much and don't want to eat them." She was only five. We thought that this may be a phase, as kids are often convinced of certain things as they grow and go through stages, but Rebecca and Spencer have never looked back and have both been strict vegetarians for the past four years. Family and friends have learned to cater for their dietary preference at lunches or dinner parties. They have even had to make a habit out of reading the labels on sweets before thinking of buying them as a treat, making sure there is no gelatine in the ingredients or the kids won't put their mouths to it.

It is, of course, easier for children to see the thin line between right and wrong and to tow this line. It is easier for them to make changes and stick to their convictions. They are still unspoilt by the influences of this world. It is for this reason that I often stop to listen to them, and try my best to see the world from their viewpoint rather than through my own "experienced" but conditioned eyes.

Chapter 5

Companionship

It was easy to get Lazarus back into his enclosure. He obediently followed us wherever we went. Brendan put his meal for the rest of the day inside his pen and he jumped in after it. His day by the river was cause for great excitement and he was completely spent by the end of it. We started packing the Land Rover, getting ready to leave, when Lazarus suddenly stopped eating and stood by the fence of his enclosure staring at us.

Rebecca dropped everything she had in her hands onto the sand and ran over to him. She could feel the intensity of his gaze; it was as if he wanted to tell us something. He pushed his little hand through the wire mesh and Rebecca reached out with an open palm. Lazzy gently placed his hand in hers and stared at her with soulful eyes. Brendan playfully told him that it was time for him to go and rest, and we reluctantly got into the Land Rover, all feeling a bit downhearted to leave.

Lazzy continued to stand by the fence, and when he realised that we were really leaving, he started making weeping noises, climbing up and down the side of his enclosure. It was clear that he did not want us to go. Rebecca could not stand the intensity of his misery and so she burst into tears herself. "We can't leave him," she pleaded with her dad, and we decided to stay until the sun had set. Lazzy settled down afterwards and found a cosy spot to sleep.

Later that evening, while relaxing in our treetop bath erected on a wooden platform in an enormous marula tree, Brendan and I pondered over the events of the day. We do most of our thinking in the bath; it's the only place where there are no other distractions needing our attention! It had taken all our willpower not to load Lazarus up and bring him home with us. His affectionate behaviour made it difficult for us to keep our distance as we normally would with other wild animals.

We were concerned over Lazzy's dependency on us, not only for survival but for companionship. Although most of the information available described the Cape clawless otter as a generally solitary animal, we could not help but feel worried that Lazarus would grow lonely if left by himself. The pained expression on his face when he realised that we were about to leave stuck with me. His reaction was similar to that of a loving family dog, only more expressive and intense. We wondered if his close relationship with humans from a young age had influenced this behaviour and set him apart from his wild counterparts. Was it possible to transfer human emotion onto a captive animal as a form of social learning?

We have often noticed that wild animals that have had contact with humans react differently, sometimes completely inconsistently, with their species' true nature. Upon further research, I found a paper published by the American Society of Mammalogists with evidence that, although exceedingly rare, Cape clawless otters have indeed been observed and documented as living in family groups of up to five. This gave us hope that Lazzy's behaviour could be normal, and that it would be natural for an otter of this species to form strong bonds. The ideal scenario was to find another captive-raised otter, pair the two up and then release them together, but we had no such luck. Lazzy would have to do dating the old-fashioned way.

Some time after this, a woman sent us a video of an otter swimming in the Hartbeespoort Dam. She lives on an estate near the water and claims that she often sees five otters playing on an island in the dam, but the night she took the video there was only one. In the video, the otter can be seen playing and foraging in shallow water. We were hopeful that one day soon, Lazzy would also join up with his own kind and have a family of his own.

The Three Sides of an Otter

By Brendan Murray

There are three sides to Mr Lazzy. First, we have the grumpy side, and that is when he is hungry. A hungry otter is a grumpy otter. And in no uncertain terms, with growls and snarls, he will let you know that he is not in the mood for tickles or playing or swimming. Just feed him.

Then he has a playful side. Clawless otters are notoriously playful, especially if their tummies are full. I could spend up to six hours a day swimming and exploring with him. Danelle always says I am just a grown-up kid, so swimming with Lazzy for the whole day was quite easy for me. I felt no guilt that I should have been working instead. After all, this is my job.

Lazzy has a third side. Lazy bones, or as we liked to call him, Lazzy Bones. When playtime was finished and he was not hungry, then it was time to nap. And no amount of coercion could keep him from his slumber, even dead in the middle of the day.

Lazzy holds onto a fish with his human-like fingers, to munch on it

After much persuasion, Lazzy finally follows Brendan into the river.

Lazzy explorers the shallow parts of the river and finds molluscs to snack on. His enclosure can be seen in the background.

Lazzy pleads with Rebecca to stay.

Chapter 6

The Great Escape

Later that evening we received a call from Godfrey.

Godfrey Sithole is a young Zimbabwean who relocated to South Africa when he was only 17 years old in search of employment, as have many others because of Zimbabwe's economic crash. We met him through Tyron, and his love for animals made him an obvious choice for assistance with this project. Godfrey refers to himself as a "zoophilist," an animal lover who concerns himself with the protection of defenseless animals.

"I love animals. I help them when they can't help themselves," he once told me. He grew up in a rural area in Manicaland Province in eastern Zimbabwe, in a village near the Sabi River. "We were surrounded by beautiful trees and wild animals. I would go down to the river and spend time there, watching the animals come to drink water. It became my hobby."

Zimbabwe is a country with exquisite natural heritage, so alluring that its national anthem celebrates its loveliness: *"Tarisai Zimbabwe, nyika yakashongedzwa. Namakomo, nehova, zvinoyevedza."* (O lovely Zimbabwe, so wondrously adorned. With mountains, and rivers cascading, flowing free.) The Sabi River where Godfrey grew up, or better known as the Save River by the local community, is a 647-km-long river that flows through Zimbabwe and Mozambique. To the locals, this is a sacred river and many stories are told about it. From mystical mermaids they refer to as *njuzu*, ancestral messengers who can both possess you and bless you with great knowledge, to the Save's tempestuous anger during flood season. The river also provides sustenance to its people, by means of fish and irrigation for crops and fruit plantations, and is therefore worshipped by all who live there.

Godfrey told me about his life in Zimbabwe as far back as he could remember. As a seven-year-old boy he had many pets, including cats, ducks, dogs and chickens. He lost his parents around the same age and found comfort in the relationship he had with his animals. He was only 10 when he got his first job as a shepherd.

"I learned that making sure animals have food, water, and shelter is only half the battle. The other half is making them feel loved. I spent a lot of time petting, grooming, and playing with my pets every day. I would speak to them in soothing tones and be there to comfort them when they were sick or scared."

During Lazarus's release, Godfrey lived on the release farm, a setting that took him back in memory to the place of his youth, and was responsible for Lazzy when we were not around. When he phoned that night, he had panic in his voice.

It was to inform us that Lazzy had escaped from his enclosure. All around the enclosure, we had dug the fence 60 cm deep into the ground when erecting his pen to make sure that he could not dig his way out. The entire area was covered but for one tiny part in the corner where the ground was uneven, and a rock obstructed the spot where we had to dig down to bury the mesh. Here, we thought, the rock would discourage any tunneling activity. But it did not take this clever otter long to realise that if he could get around the rock, he could break free. The earlier separation from us had upset him enough to spark his brain into action.

When Godfrey rode his bicycle down to the river where the enclosure stood to check on Lazarus, he found the otter walking along the dirt road, sniffing and prancing ahead. Lazzy was used to being in an enclosure. He grew up in captivity, and as far as we know he had never tried to escape before. What made him want to break out that night we will never really know. Was it his exposure to the outside world earlier in the day? Did the river and his natural habitat prompt it? Or was his plan to come and find us?

Godfrey managed to coax him back into his enclosure without any trouble. He closed up the exit hole Lazarus had made for himself and made sure that he was secure for the night. But Lazzy's escape had us worried - so much so that neither of us got any sleep that night. We left the house before sunrise the next day to go meet with Godfrey and to inspect the enclosure for any other weak spots. Boy, did we underestimate the intelligence of this otter!

If Godfrey had not found Lazarus when he did, the outcome could have been disastrous. Lazzy was not ready to be on his own. He had not familiarised himself with his surroundings, nor established a territory, nor even learned how to feed himself. He was petrified of swimming, so how could he possibly survive by himself? What would happen when he encountered predators such as crocodiles, which were a real threat in this river? All these dreadful thoughts kept drifting around in my mind. For a brief moment I contemplated our determination to set Lazzy free. Had we made the right decision to take this project on? Would he not be safer in captivity?

After we arrived, we let Lazarus out of his enclosure and took him down to the river. I only had to see him for a short while, relishing in his new-found and unquestionable freedom, to know that we could make no other decision. We had to see him through this; we had to help Lazarus return to the wild. As the saying goes: "A ship is safe in a harbour, but that is not what ships are built for." We may be able to protect an animal in captivity, and they may even live longer lives, but what quality of existence can we give over the life Nature intended for them?

In our own lives, Brendan and I have always believed in living a satisfying life, rich with experience, over a safe and guarded one that has little meaning. We are adventurous in our endeavours, bold in our decisions, and fearless in our pursuits. We could have spent our lives in a security estate, working a sensible nine-to-five job, earning a stable salary, climbing the proverbial ladder of success and would have gotten zero fulfilment from it. Or we could live in the moment, make a difference, shed a tear but know we tried, and do what sets our spirits free. To keep an animal in captivity would go against every grain of our being. However, we had to be sure that Lazarus was not going to escape again before his teachings were complete.

We spent hours making changes and upgrades to the release enclosure. We packed the entire floor area around the edges of the enclosure with concrete bricks, making excavating an escape route an impossibility. This time, we were certain that we had his confinement covered. To be even more sure, we camped out next to his enclosure that night to observe Lazzy's night-time behaviour. To watch the burning red sun being swallowed up by the horizon on the banks of the river is a treat, and I could easily be left there for days. The remoteness appeased my soul. Before the fish eagles greeted the day with a final call and the owls sat high in the trees hooting, Lazarus had made himself comfortable to go to sleep.

Whether it was his eventful pursuit to escape the night before that had him worn out, or our presence giving him comfort, he was peacefully asleep for most of the night. The sound of the rushing river was like a lullaby soothing me into a slumber, and by 10:00 I could hardly keep my eyes open. Brendan sat up by the fire for another few hours before he was content that Lazarus would not be active until daybreak.

I woke refreshed the next morning. The wilderness air had me feeling energised. The sound of the African bushveld woke me at first light as the pair of fish eagles, whose nest was less than 100 m from Lazzy's enclosure, flew overhead. Their calls echoed through the valley as they followed the river upstream, looking for their morning catch. The distance to the chalet camp where a hot shower awaited was a long stretch of dirt road along the river, weaving through tall trees. As I walked, I inhaled the fresh air and felt as if I had become aware of the breath inside my lungs for the very first time. The vervet monkeys shouted insults from the trees, and I felt like the new kid at school who was still being mocked as an outsider. Their curious faces peeked over the branches as they inspected this stranger in their territory.

After a luxurious shower (well, the fact that it had hot running water made it luxurious to me in that setting), I returned with water for our morning cup of coffee, which we made in a blackened steel kettle on the fire. It was not long before I was again covered in river slush and otter prints decorating my otherwise clean clothes. Lazzy was ready and eager for another day of exploring.

Chapter 7

Swept Away

As the days passed, Lazarus ventured more and more into the shallows of the river. The kids had a royal time joining in his fun of foraging for freshwater mussels and chasing after crabs. He gladly accepted their gifts of mollusc treats and crunched on them insatiably. We had been placing his food in the water trough inside his enclosure to slowly get him used to dipping his head under water to forage or hunt for food. He eagerly dived in after fish we placed in the bath. He would pull and drag a 1-kg catfish out to eat it in a comfortable spot on the sand, but take it back to the water several times in between bites to rinse it clean.

In the river, he would now do the same. He walked along in the shallows looking for whatever he could find to pick at and nibble on. When he was given a big fish to chomp on, he would find a spot along the riverbank where he could lie flat on his tummy and enjoy his meal. He reminded me of a toddler with an ice-cream cone, with both of his hands tightly gripped around the fish. Sure enough, in between he would run up to the water's edge and dip his fish in the river to rinse it clean of sand.

When the news got out that we were working with a Cape clawless otter and teaching him to be wild, a whole community of people offered their help. Local fishermen saved buckets of fish for Lazzy, fish farms donated their surplus, and the local little restaurant in town, Fisherman's Deck, made sure that there was always a pail of fish available for the well-loved otter. Food was in no short supply. Once a week we would drive around in our open-roof Land Rover collecting the live catfish and tilapia in buckets of water with nets over them to keep the fish from jumping out, spilling water everywhere and mist spraying into our faces from the wind as we drove back to the farm.

Lazzy was running and splashing through the shallow water near the sandbank when he noticed Brendan a few metres away, swimming in the deeper part of the river to cool off from the scorching sun. The inquisitive otter perked up with excitement, stood up on his hind legs to get a better view, and then bravely swam over to him. This was his first time entering water that required swimming, which was vastly different than the shallow waters he was used to and which he could easily walk through. Lazzy completely underestimated the current of the river. He unexpectedly found himself in deep water and had to rely on his undeveloped swimming skills to get him across to where Brendan was.

The fast-flowing water overwhelmed the otter as it swept him further and further down the river and away from Brendan. Lazzy cried out in shrill shrieks as he continued downstream. I called to him, trying to persuade him to swim over to my side, back to the sandbank and shallow waters. It would have been closer for him to turn back to me and far easier to exit the water, but the headstrong otter was determined to keep going in the direction he had planned on going. He was intent on getting to Brendan, one way or another, even if it terrified him.

Brendan couldn't keep up with him in the river and his only option was to swim to the side, climb out onto the bank, which on that side was high and covered with foliage and roots, and follow Lazzy along on land, coaxing him to swim towards him to the side of the river where he would be able to escape onto the bank. Lazarus made it to the bank, but the edge was too steep for him to exit and he slipped right back into the water. Spencer, worried that Lazzy may drown or be swept away never to be seen again, promptly and without any hesitation or consideration for his own safety, jumped in and followed behind him in the river, eager to lend a hand to the little otter he had grown very fond of. Hereafter both Spencer and Lazarus were at the mercy of the river.

The river, by good fortune, reached another sandbank further downstream where the water was shallow, and the pair were washed up onto an island. Brendan could spot the sandbank ahead and, battling his way through thick greenery, managed to meet them there. The trio walked across to the riverbank, with only a narrow portion of river left to get through before climbing to safety. Lazzy hesitated for a moment to re-enter the water so soon after his ordeal, but with Brendan on one side and Spencer on the other, they were able to dispel his fears and he followed their lead. He had put all his trust in them and they crossed the section of river side by side. Once they reached the bank, Spencer gave Lazzy a small nudge to help him up the steep slope onto the pathway that ran along the bank.

The three of them re-joined Rebecca and me shortly after. Lazarus came and lay down a few metres from me, rolling around on his back to dry himself on the coarse sweltering river sand. In that moment he reminded me so much of our family dogs who were waiting for us back home, and I realised just how attached we had grown to Lazzy.

A deep emotional connection forms between a human and an animal in this type of scenario, a bond that is unlike any other. The relationship between an animal and a person is without prejudice, it is unconditional, it is kind, it is complete, and it is infinite. Animals do not care for our accomplishments, our appearance, or our social status. They love and trust effortlessly. The love that can exist between an animal and a human is therefore both pure and unreserved. When you are loved by an animal, you truly experience the meaning of love. It is not so strange, then, that there are many non-profit organisations, psychologists, social workers, and therapists who use animals in their treatment methods to combat depression, self-consciousness, and anxiety with great success.

When I was a child, I was an extreme introvert. I felt that I was constantly being judged by those around me. I was the quiet girl, too afraid to speak. I believed that if I could be mostly invisible, then nobody would notice my imperfections. I believed that I needed to be perfect to be loved. This, of course, is unobtainable to anyone, and as a result I suffered from very low self-esteem. To overcome this, I turned to animals and nature for comfort. I soon realised that my dogs loved me exactly the way I was, no matter what. And it seemed as though they listened attentively as I shared all my stories of things that troubled me. Among the trees and in the wild outdoors, I felt like I belonged to a world absent of the harshness of everyday life. I could be myself, without fear or trepidation, when I was among animals. My dogs became my therapists.

My stillness meant that my focus was on listening and observing. I became skilled at reading social cues that would come to help me throughout my life. As I grew and developed, I finally found coping mechanisms and acceptance of myself through the study of life forms around me. Animals shaped my thoughts and changed the way I viewed the world. I realised that even the smallest, simplest single-cell living being had a purpose and the power to influence the world. If not for the microscopically tiny bacteria in the soil that are responsible for decomposing materials and creating energy in the Earth's food web, plants would not be able to grow. Even though they are small, and seem insignificant and completely invisible to most, they are, as it happens, a big deal.

In working closely with Lazzy, we developed an extraordinarily strong affection for him; it was impossible not to. Lessons he taught us, through just being who he is, would serve as perfect metaphors in our own lives and would leave a life-long impression on us. Lazzy was brave and enthusiastic to learn new things, which taught us not to fear change. Life is all about perspective and having a positive outlook can make all the difference. You do not go into a project like this, working with an animal like Lazarus, and come out unchanged. Every day he would open my eyes to something new. He gave us a new perspective not only on our own lives but on ways we could improve the world around us and the environment we live in.

In the back of my mind, though, I could never brush off the thought that the day would come when we would have to say goodbye. Today he had seemed so vulnerable in the river, calling out to us, depending on us to rescue him. I wanted to scoop him up, take him in my arms, and comfort him. I wanted to assure him that everything would be okay. Our intention of freeing him to live in the wild and to fend for himself was still a terrifying thought. This decision to help re-wild an otter came with daily reflection on the best possible outcome for Lazarus, which in moments of occasional doubt caused both Brendan and me a fair deal of anxiety.

Setting Boundaries

By Brendan Murray

Once we had introduced Lazzy to his new environment, we decided we needed to put a couple of boundaries in place. We wanted him to be able to explore the river and its banks to his heart's content, but within an area that we could monitor. So, every morning at sunrise I would walk upriver with him to a man-made weir, then I would dive in with Lazzy following right behind.

This section of the Crocodile River is around 40 m at its widest and 15 m at its narrowest. The shallow end is knee-deep and the deepest part we found was just over 4 m deep (when it's not raining). It's an easy swim. As soon as you get to the deep part, the current takes you quite quickly and you just need to float on your back with your legs and feet up, so you don't get tangled up in a submerged log. As the river winds through the valley, the deeper part snakes from the left bank through the middle and onto the right bank and back again.

Lazzy would tumble and spin and explore the riverbed, but as soon as he noticed I was too far away he would anxiously swim to catch up. We decided that a 5-km stretch of the river would suffice, which on a good day would take about an hour-and-a-half to swim. Once we reached that mark, we would make our way up the riverbank and take the 5-km walk back to the weir. Most days we would undertake this adventure twice. On other days we would do it just once, but on rainy days the level of the water could rise over 5 m, making it way too dangerous to go in.

With Lazarus being relatively cautious, we noticed that when we left him to explore by himself and with us just watching from a distance, he never once went past the weir. We had managed to create an invisible boundary. If he had decided to just take off, the Crocodile River flows 600 km north to the Botswana border, where it joins up with the Marico River, changes its name to the Limpopo, and then flows along the Zimbabwe border, passing the northernmost part of the Kruger Park and through Mozambique until it meets Xai-Xai, a little coastal village on the Indian Ocean. All in all, that would be a 1,000-km trip - quite a potential adventure, but one plagued with too many crocodiles to make it possible.

Chapter 8

Crocodile River

The water was like ice. I took short, quick breaths with each step as I made my way from the shallows near the bank and waded through to the deeper section of the river where the water came up to under my chin. Whether my rapid short breaths of air were caused by the cold water, or triggered by the intense fear I felt for what may be lurking underneath me, was unclear. On a normal day you would not get me anywhere near water this cold, much less cloudy, murky water where innumerable things could be hiding at the bottom.

My toes curled up, perturbed at the different textures. I could only guess by the feeling and sensation of each object under my sensitive feet, what I was stepping on. It was a mixture of sand, rocks, shells, weed, algae, scum, plant roots, and logs. The thought of a fish brushing up against my leg sent shivers up and down my spine.

My fear of murky water stems from childhood, and try as I may in all the years I've spent working in the wild, I have not been able to shake this phobia and my irrational fear of dark, mysterious waters. I absolutely love the ocean. I enjoy few activities as much as bathing in the sea, with its sense of freedom. I want to sail out to sea in a yacht, into the deep blue yonder, and stay there for weeks. But at the same time, it scares me half to death. I am absolutely terrified at the thought of the vast, vague, restless body of water where I harbour no control.

This stretch of the Crocodile River was just about as wild as it gets and was indeed inhabited by crocodiles, among other predators. Often, we would watch as a snake swam across from one side of the river over to the other. To unnerve me even further, a leguaan (water monitor lizard) would drop down from a tree somewhere behind me into the water, making a huge splash upon entry. At a quick glance, this large reptile, wiggling its powerful tail and body through the water, is easily mistaken for a croc.

Brendan swam and splashed in the river as if he were an otter himself, and laughed at my silly display of shakes and jitters. I was completely out of my comfort zone, yet here I was in the middle of the Crocodile

River, overcoming a whole bucketful of fears because the job required it. The brief sacrifice and discomfort would be well worth the rewards I would reap in the end. Part of the process needed for Lazarus's adaptation was to get him comfortable in his habitat by taking him for daily swims.

Animals, like people, can be taught through social learning. Learning takes place when new experiences are explored by watching and observing others perform certain tasks, and then adopting this behaviour as your own. It is a game of imitation. We have observed many examples of social learning in our work with animals. When we release owls into a new environment, we always release two or more owls together. The success rate is much higher doing this, because the owls learn from and assist each other in adapting to the new environment.

We use a release hack in most of the owl releases we do. This is an enclosure where the owls, much like Lazzy, are given the opportunity to get used to the environment around them before they are released. The hack is built where the owls have a good view of their surroundings and where they can get used to the natural elements of the area. After the usual six-week period, the hatch - a little doorway in the hack - is opened and the birds are free to leave and come back at their will.

During this stage, we have observed that most of the owls take their time to leave, cautious and almost afraid of the outside world. They have grown accustomed to the hack and it has become their base of safety. It is only when one brave owl takes the courageous flight onto the outside perch that the others follow suit. With soundless communication, they encourage each other to move forward. Within minutes of each other, all the owls decide to leave the hack and explore the world around it. And one by one they return to the hack until the next night. When they finally feel ready to brave the wider world, they leave for good to seek their own territories and to continue their life in the wild.

By going into the water ourselves, we gave Lazarus the confidence to follow in after us. This allowed him to explore the river and his new environs with the reassurance he gained through our fellowship. Lazarus, being an otter, would naturally be drawn to water and have the ability to swim, but it was as if we had to, in some way, awaken these instincts that were dormant within him. We needed to facilitate the development of his natural behaviour, an innate process he missed out on as a captive-raised otter.

A baby otter would usually learn many crucial survival skills under the safeguard of his protective mother. In the wild, an otter pup would leave the den at about four weeks old to accompany mommy on foraging excursions. This is where the pup would learn to swim by watching his mother going about her business.

It amazed me how quickly Lazarus got over his ordeal of being swept away by the current. He did not dwell on it for even a minute. He accepted it as the learning curve it was. The next time he entered the river, he knew exactly where the shallow parts ended and where the sandbank dipped into the deep water. He understood the current better and practiced swimming where he felt safe. Before long, he had mastered the skill. Animals are natural survivalists. They take on every task as if their life depended on that very thing (and more often than not it does). Lazzy had an indomitable spirit to overcome obstacles, which would serve him well in his life ahead.

Lazarus would later swim between Brendan and me, dipping his head under from time to time to see what was underneath us. By now he had gained enough confidence to dive down to pick up mussel shells off the riverbed. His fingers would feel around the bottom of the river, gently touching on the sand, searching for mollusks or crabs to nibble on. The Cape clawless otter is the only one of the 13 species of otters found around the world that has no claws and hardly any nails. His adept little fingers moved quickly, disturbing the sand underneath us while grabbing at food.

In later months when he grew more comfortable in the water and had had enough to eat, he would turn this into a game rather than a foraging exercise. Instead of looking for food to eat, he would dive to grab at my toes, wiggling them between his fingers, before popping back up. Within seconds he would be over at Brendan's side doing the same. In the murky water, it was impossible to see him coming - you just felt a sudden tickle on your toes. It would take me by surprise each and every time, and I would either giggle or yelp; I never got used to the strange sensation. His fingers were like a monkey's - small, strong, and coarse. (Brendan said they were the hands of a dwarf bricklayer.) The more self-assured Lazzy became in the water, the more playful he became, and grabbing at our toes was a favourite source of amusement.

After a while I managed to calm my nerves and enter a state of mindful meditation to overcome my anxiety about going into the water. Over time, the fear subsided and turned into a feeling of exhilaration. In that moment, every one of my senses was aroused by the environment around me and I could take everything in in full. You transcend into wonderment in a wild place like this - a sensation that never weakens, no matter how much time you spend in Nature's company. I stood in amazement at the beauty that surrounded me. The cool water rushed past my body, gently pushing and pulling at me, releasing the tension from my strained muscles. It was the most natural feeling of contentment I had ever experienced. My mind was completely clear of any other thoughts and I was entirely engulfed in the moment. Discomfort turned to something strangely satisfying. The calmness of the water spilled over into my soul; I am in love with the wild world.

Pushing myself beyond my comfort zone to allow the strangeness of the environment in, along with its beauty, felt as good as a holiday. I felt so far removed from the world of busy traffic, noise, and pollution. Like Lazzy, I too felt in my own way as if I had returned to where I was meant to be. My mind no longer felt suffocated by the meaningless stimulation it is filled with daily as a by-product of living in modern society. It was for once perfectly still. The greenery, the tranquil water, and fresh air carries the soul to another dimension.

After our swim, we gave Lazzy a large catfish for lunch, which he carried tightly gripped in his jaws. His head was tilted slightly backward, forming a small arch in his back, and his nose was lifted in the air, like a peasant with newly acquired wealth, as his short legs trotted up the embankment with it. The head of the fish was hanging out on the left side of his mouth and the tail was sticking out on the right side; the fish was so big that it almost dragged on the ground on either side of Lazarus!

To our surprise, he ran straight up to his enclosure to wash his fish in the large water trough. When he was satisfied, he jumped down off the edge of the troth, ran back out through the gate and down to the riverside, all the while carrying the 2-kg fish, to finally eat it in the shade by the river. He noisily devoured the entire thing. Lazzy was so used to receiving his meals inside his enclosure, where he had become accustomed to washing and eating his food in the artificial water pool, that he obediently did the same when we gave him a fish by the river. It had become clear to us that a perplexed conflict existed in Lazzy's mind between his life in captivity and the new life that he was embarking on.

Crocodiles

By Brendan Murray

Every morning starts the same: scout up and down the river for crocodiles. If none are seen, well, then we can go fishing. Danelle probably asked me the same question every single day, "What I would do if, while swimming, I did happen to see a croc approaching?" "Swim a little faster," would be my answer. I would also joke: Just imagine how many more people would get to know about our story if it happened that one of us became lizard food?

Brendan observes as Lazzy gets used to his new environment

Lazzy enjoys delicacies from the river.

Rebecca waits for Lazzy to follow her into the water.

Spencer plays with Lazarus.

Chapter 9
Twilight

By mid-October we were in the peak time of spotted eagle owl breeding season. This is the most common owl species in South Africa and the ones we most often treat at the Sanctuary. Orphaned and abandoned babies were coming in from everywhere and before I knew it, I was tied down with four-hourly feeds of about a dozen hungry mouths. Raising baby owls is about as much work as it was raising my own human babies, except that the process is repeated several times a year. In one year alone I have raised close to 800 hatchlings of various species.

Between feeds, there is cleaning and washing to do. Their bedding is changed twice a day because of the mess they make. Baby barn owls can be moved to their release box at around 48 days, two weeks before fledging, when they are able to swallow their food whole and no longer require hand feeding. At around three weeks of age, we place the spotted eagle owl babies with foster moms, usually owls that can't be released into the wild and are permanent residents at the Sanctuary, Spotted eagle owls will adopt any baby and care for it like their own, especially during breeding season. But until they are old enough and ready for this step, it is up to Brendan and me to take on the parental role.

It was hard to find someone to help us, especially over weekends when most of our staff take time off. As much as we wanted to believe that the people we employ are here because of their passion for animals, it was clear during this time that our staff merely performed tasks to earn their pay. Besides the occasional volunteer, no one was willing to put in the hours required for raising baby birds. Finding someone to give up their time freely, to work for the satisfaction of fulfilling one's life purpose alone, is rare and felt close to impossible. We live in a competitive world and one could hardly blame a person for this. Therefore, we had no alternative but to take on the responsibility entirely by ourselves.

We were duty bound. We had an obligation toward these baby birds. We also had a commitment to Lazarus and his release process, which meant juggling our duties and taking the baby owls with us when we went to work with Lazzy. This entailed a lot of planning and put additional strain on us. We were exhausted, but the time we had with

Lazarus was well worth the trouble. He would run up to where I was feeding the baby owls, standing up on his hind legs and poking his nose into the back of the Land Rover to get a view of what was distracting me and taking up so much of my time. I had to be careful not to allow him anywhere near them. He stood there like a nagging toddler until I was ready to join in the fun at the river.

As the weeks progressed, Lazarus had grown closer to the environment around him and his behaviour mimicked that of a wild otter more and more as time went by. He was marking a territory for himself that involved a comic little dance. With his front paws steady in position to bear his full weight, he bounced from side to side on his back legs with his tail up in the air, quickly shifting sides; wiggling his behind left and right, he sprayed faeces at the latrine sites he had chosen. Whether he knew to do this to communicate his presence to other Cape clawless otters in the area, or if he did it to attract a female, was unclear.

He was also exploring dens, natural cavities found along the riverbank that were probably made by other animals like warthogs, or digging in the banks to make his own. In his life, Lazzy had never been taught by another otter to burrow or to mark his territory. This behaviour was guided only by instinct - knowledge that is known through his genetic ancestry alone. It was as if a memory had been awakened from a life he had lived before this one. All he needed was the time to rediscover this memory for himself, and we were merely there to facilitate this process.

The days grew warmer and he became less active at midday when the sun was at its hottest. His activity peaked during the twilight hours - dawn and dusk - which was another sign that he was adapting to his environment by avoiding the scorching heat of the region by becoming crepuscular. Our days stretched longer and longer. We were so busy between rescues, rearing owlets and working with Lazarus, that the days seemed to all melt into one.

The extra hours of work did not bother me one bit, and I would not have noticed how hard we had been working if it were not for the trouble that was about to come. It was the actions of an antagonist who has had it in for us for several years that had me feeling worn out and tired. I knew that it was her intention to debilitate us, and so I refused to let it get me under and decided to instead focus my attention on a positive outcome.

Chapter 10

An Anonymous Complaint

When we started working with wildlife full-time, it was to fulfil a need, not only for wildlife to be protected but also a need within ourselves. Brendan and I are both philosophical by nature, and we craved to spend our time doing something that carried meaning. I suppose that everyone wants the same basic thing: we want to be happy in this life and somehow find a way to make that happiness last.

Someone once told me that the purpose of life is not to be happy but simply to have a purpose. Working for a cause is the key to unlocking happiness, and you make that happiness last by leaving a legacy. For some, this means creating beautiful artworks people can marvel at. Some make music that touches the soul, while others influence the world through poems and stories. Architects and construction workers create buildings and homes which dreams are built on. Farmers grow food and provide nourishment. Meaning and purpose is found in procreation, too. Having kids and transferring our knowledge to them is the most basic way in which we leave a legacy. In all this, we find a way to live forever, to carry our memory long after we are gone.

Brendan and I had reached a defining point in our lives when we decided to focus all our attention on protecting owls. It was one of those rare opportunities when life pushes you down so hard that the only thing left to do is to give in and make a change. A day comes when a caterpillar stops eating, hangs upside down from a twig, and spins itself a cocoon. Then on a specific day, it accepts change and is ready to morph into a butterfly. We stopped worrying about money and about earthly possessions, things that brought us little joy and were easily lost; they would only leave us feeling empty. Instead, we decided to dedicate our lives to saving owls.

Making such a decision is no easy feat, especially when you come from a family where high value is placed on making money. My dad is a businessman, and instead of running a charity himself he has donated thousands of rands to charities over the years. His dad, my grandfather, did the same. They made an abundance of money for themselves and gave a percentage away to others in need.

When the time came for me to pick a career, I told my dad that I wanted to be an artist. I considered studying Fine Art when I left school. I had spent most of my holidays painting birds or animals in watercolours and later dabbled in a variety of mediums, such as charcoal drawings and acrylic paints. This, I suppose, is where my elementary observation of birds and wildlife started. To sketch and paint something, you need to study and have appreciation for your subject. I dreamt of capturing the true beauty of nature on canvas.

My dad told me simply, "There is no money to be made as an artist," and I should set my sights on something else. And so I did. For years I worked at different jobs, trying to find something that would satisfy me. I strived to achieve self-actualization. But something was missing from my life. The work seemed bottomless, like a deep pit I was throwing myself and my time into, with no end goal in mind.

Brendan and I enjoy travelling, hiking, and exploring the countryside. We love the great outdoors and our fondness for nature is probably what brought us together in the first place and forged our strong connection. In time, our concern for wildlife and the environment grew stronger, and when we stood at the proverbial crossroads in our lives, a career in conservation became an obvious choice. This meant giving up any chance at becoming wealthy. My friends would get to drive fancy cars, wear expensive clothes, sip on cocktails, and live on large estates, while I would spend my time in khaki pants in the bush. They would get to fly to exotic destinations for holidays while I camped in a Land Rover next to a river.

None of that fazed me. I had long realised that wealth has many faces, and as a conservationist and a writer I would have happiness in abundance; my wealth would be in the form of passion for my work. There would be hard times, harder than one could imagine. I would shed many tears over the pain, death, and destruction I witnessed in this line of work. There would be times of utter frustration in the fight against cruelty. At times I'd feel utter hopelessness, despair, and despondency. But these fleeting times of desperation, during which I would nearly concede defeat, are quickly dissolved by the next opportunity to heal, reintegrate, and set free.

We knew that there was a need to protect owls, and this was the deciding factor behind the birth of Owl Rescue Centre. We did not pick owls because we liked them more than other animals. We focused our attention on the conservation of owls because they needed our protection more than any other creature at that point in time. Owls were dying on the roads because they so often get hit by cars; poison was being used indiscriminately to control rodents but killing owls and other animals too; and superstitious beliefs meant that owls were persecuted and killed. Owls have an exceptionally high mortality rate and without intervention their population will dwindle. We were set on making a difference and we succeeded. Over the years we have seen an increase in owl populations and a positive change in people's perceptions and behaviour. More and more people are realising the dangers of rodent poisons and we now get daily inquiries seeking our advice on protecting and safeguarding owls.

Back in 2014 when our organisation had started to become more well-known and popular within the public and wildlife sphere, and more and more cases came flooding in, one organisation in particular - or rather, the person who headed up that organisation at the time - turned malevolent towards us. She was involved with a project in which anyone with enough money (which included a long list of companies, schools, housing estates, and private individuals) could purchase owls for release at their own premises as a method of controlling rodents. Those who bought into this scheme were almost always good-hearted conservation-conscious people who, inadvertently, had a hand in what is essentially, in our opinion, wildlife trading. There were also those who simply saw the owls as a solution to a rodent problem, or as a good PR exercise for their company or establishment.

We were against the project for many reasons, but the process of the release - the lack of expert control over the release (which was, for the most part, left in the hands of the general public) as well as the absence of post-release monitoring of the owls were some of our main concerns. We were speaking from experience, as we had to intervene and rescue many of these releases that went wrong. It came to the point where we thought it necessary to raise our concerns with those responsible. We invited them to meet with us, to sit around a table and discuss our concerns for the owls, but were met by a belligerent attitude toward our viewpoint. They never attended the suggested meeting and the project continued irrespective.

The organization locked young barn owls inside small boxes for weeks, to be released once they were fully fledged (with all their adult feathers in place). There was no scope for these owls to gain fitness or become familiar with their surroundings pre-release, and we felt that their natural development would be stunted in the process. These owls would likely be incapable of hunting, and their chances of survival would be slim. The birds were traded like a commodity - a simple pest-control business transaction with little consciousness and regard for the well-being of the owls themselves. We noticed how people's perceptions of owls changed from the wild creatures they are to something that could now be bought and owned to serve an intended purpose.

The process of the release was passed on to any person who paid for the "rights" to the owls. There were no criteria guiding where these owls would be released. They were often placed in areas that posed a danger to them, where superstitious beliefs about owls are still prevalent, because the city council would be willing to pay a fortune for the service of these owls. On paper it looked great for them, using a "natural pest control agent," but in reality, the project was a total failure. We were called in to rescue several owls that had been persecuted and injured.

In another instance, a company that had purchased owls from this organisation gave their security guard the responsibility of feeding them while the owls remained in their small box "preparing for release." One employee became concerned about the well-being of the owls when they noticed a terrible stench coming from the box. The guard, who was uninterested in the project but had been tasked with their feeding, had emptied the entire bag of day-old chicks into the box on the first day and left them with "enough food" to last them the four-week period they were meant to stay in the box. The day-old chickens had started to rot, as a result of the overfeeding and by the time the box was broken open to rescue the owls, the box was crawling with maggots. Only two of the three owls that were inside the box survived and were treated for emaciation and dehydration.

We tried to discuss the shortcomings of this project with the organisation in question, but to no avail. However, the more rescues we did, the less access they had to owls for this project, which turned over hundreds of thousands of rands each year. This prevented any chance of a courteous relationship between us. A public battle broke out and the media became involved. The project in question is still operational, but the person who ran the original organisation, which closed their doors in

2015, has since opened a new wildlife rehabilitation entity from which we suspect owls are now sourced for this project.

As a result, we believe they have tried to cause the downfall of our organisation for several years. The animosity is so immense that the same person along with her new business partner even tried to interfere with Lazzy's release, by contacting the Department of Nature Conservation with a complaint to have him taken from our care.

Dr. Schouwstra had first found our details while searching for a place that could take in two spotted eagle owls. We had been operating the Owl Sanctuary for about 10 years when Brendan met with Dr. Schouwstra and showed her around the place. The owls she had to re-home had been in her care for some time and she had obvious sentiment for them. She was picky about where they would go. It was not an easy decision for her to leave them with someone else, but something told her that surrendering them to us was the right decision to make for them. Over time she got to know us better and followed our work closely. She called on us for favours whenever the need emerged, either to transport wildlife in need of care or to help with a rescue. So when she needed help with Lazarus, she knew that she could rely on us to assist with his release.

Our speciality no doubt is working with owls. We have been working with owl species for over a decade, spending every day of our lives either rescuing, rehabilitating, releasing, or just studying them, which amounted to dealing with thousands of owls over the years. This, however, does not mean that we would not do everything we could to help another animal. Our love for animals runs deep throughout all species and we shift our focus to where we are needed. The principles of wildlife rehabilitation remain largely the same, and we can easily apply our knowledge and experience to all wildlife, with some obvious variations in methods and care. When asked, we confidently took on the task of seeing to the otter's release. We knew that Dr. Schouwstra had exhausted all her options and, without our help, there was little chance that Lazarus would ever experience freedom.

During Lazzy's release process, he became quite the media star. He was popular with news outlets from all over the world. We felt fortunate to be working with such a special animal and we wanted to share his progress with everyone. We knew there were many people who shared our desire to see him go free, so we published updates on Facebook for others to share in our joy. The response we received was incredible. The public simply loved him. With every update, more and more people joined in to follow his journey. This was the perfect opportunity to create awareness about Cape clawless otters, another animal species that is often persecuted, and we decided to make the most of it.

It was about two months into the release process, after a video of Lazarus swimming in the river received a good deal of attention, that we received an unexpected phone call from our local Department of Nature Conservation inspection unit. The complainant, who had asked to remain anonymous, claimed that we did not have the necessary permits to work with an otter. By law, the Department must investigate any matter brought to them and a meeting had to be arranged.

For us to work with wildlife, we need to apply for separate permits for literally everything we do. A permit is issued to allow us to "keep an animal," even just temporarily for the purpose of rehabilitating an injured animal on the mend. Another permit is required for "handling" wildlife, which would include picking an animal up, moving it, or rescuing it. Then there is a permit required for "transporting" wildlife from one site to another (for example, taking it from the place where it was injured to a veterinary practice). This process is further complicated with import and export permits, where each province that is crossed while transporting an animal has to issue you with a permit to bring the animal into the province or to take the animal out.

The average person on the street is blissfully unaware of all of these laws. They are unintentionally broken daily by people with good intentions wanting to save a life. Unfortunately, these people are not professionally involved in wildlife care. As a wildlife rehabilitation facility, we are strongly governed by these regulations (which are in place to protect our wildlife), and should we be found in breach of the legislation, we could be fined, closed down, or barred from working with wildlife altogether.

We knew straight away who the complainant was, and our suspicion was later confirmed in a public statement made by her. The complaint was not made out of concern for the well-being of Lazarus - it was obvious from the video that he was doing well - but rather out of spite, to settle an old score.

We had to write a report about our work with Lazarus and submit this to the Department. They also wanted all the details about our collaboration with Dr. Schouwstra.

After the meeting with the representatives of the North West Department of Nature Conservation was concluded, we packed up to go spend the night with Lazzy. My hands trembled as I carelessly and helter-skelter stuffed bags with clothing and the bare necessities. I was upset over the unpleasantness of it all and felt emotionally exhausted from all the worry. Brendan thought that spending the night in the outdoors, close to Lazzy, would be the perfect distraction. Besides, we had planned to start with his practice of catching a fish early the next morning. I could not wait to get to him. I felt the need to see him, to look him in the eyes, and to make a promise to him: that we would protect him no matter what. Brendan and I would in a heartbeat risk everything to protect those we love.

We arrived on the release farm just after midday. After we had finished what we had planned to accomplish for the day, to dam up a section of the river, we made a fire by the riverside and boiled some water for coffee. I had always believed that a cup of coffee enjoyed out there in the wilderness could remedy almost anything, but the uneasy feeling of the meeting earlier that day clung to my body like a wet set of clothes. It was a clear night and the gleaming stars were bright overhead.

After the kids had gone to bed, Brendan and I had a long discussion and agreed that even if we were asked to, we would not hand Lazzy over - not this far in his process, and not after the progress he had shown in his new environment. We could not help but feel disquieted about the situation and the possible outcomes, even though I could see that the Nature Conservation inspectors were on our side. A part of me wished that I could stay out here with Lazzy forever, and forget about the world and its issues.

In conclusion of the investigation, no contravention could be found, and we were cleared to continue with our work. Our rival's complaint was nothing more than a fly in the ointment.

I did not mind one bit that I had to write the report for the Department. In fact, I was so proud of what we had accomplished with Lazarus and the progress that he had made that I relished sharing this information in an extensive document detailing our findings. It was the thought that someone with such malicious intentions toward us could jeopardise the future of Lazarus that pained me. Had the Department of Nature Conservation given in to her demands, they could have confiscated Lazzy. Had they further acted on the suggestion that Lazarus was a tame apex predator too dangerous for release, he would have ended up either in a zoo or worse, euthanised.

When we mentioned the complaint to Dr. Schouwstra and told her who had been responsible for it, she was flabbergasted. What we did not know up until that moment is that the complainant was the same person who had originally rescued Lazarus, but who had passed the buck to Dr. Schouwstra a few years ago! The same person who had taken so little interest in his release when she had the opportunity was the very person who had tried to have him taken away from our protection. I can appreciate that she may have had good reasons why she could not assist in securing a release spot when the time came, when he was old enough to go free, or that she wasn't in a position to see to the release herself. Circumstances may not have allowed for it. I know far too little about it for me to pass judgement.

What unsettled me was the criticism we received from her and her organisation about our involvement, and the doom-laden prophecies about his chances of a successful reintroduction into the wild. She had no grounds to make such bold statements that could have had an impact on his entire future, especially as she had had no dealings with him in his later years. I would have expected her to approach us directly to discuss the project instead of running to the authorities, hoping for the worst possible outcome, when she knew that a permit was a mere formality. She could have afforded that kind of decency at least, if not for us then for Lazzy.

Not long after this, a few months at most, we heard an announcement that her organisation was caring for two baby otters. One had been flown all the way from East London to Johannesburg by a pilot known to us, to receive "specialised" care. We were actually in East London on a project when the baby otter was found. We received a call about him that very day. Also a boy like Lazzy, he had been placed in the care of the Aquarium after he washed out on the rocks. We drove to the curator's house to meet with her and to see if we could be of assistance. The animal was in perfect health and our advice was to take him back to the beach where he was found and to wait there with him for his mother to fetch him. He was not injured or sick - just misplaced. If it were up to us, we would have camped out on the beach to see to the family's reunion. There must have been other factors at play that we were not aware of that made it impossible to reunite the family and left no other option but to raise him in a wildlife rehabilitation facility. Instead of joining his family back in the wild on a beach in the Eastern Cape, he landed up in Johannesburg.

In social media posts that followed, supporters of both organisations suggested that the female otter join Lazarus at his release site. One well-meaning message read: "Owl Rescue Centre has rehabilitated a young male. Can your girl not be released there?" and another comment read in response: "I was going to say the same thing. We could soon see baby Lazaruses." But our rival's organisation responded by shutting down the idea and claimed to be better skilled and specialised to see to Lazzy's release themselves. "It would probably be best then if that otter came to our facility," she stated.

We simply shrugged it off. If this was indeed the case, why did she not get involved in his release all those years back when she not only had the opportunity but also the moral duty to see to his release. Was what they had said in a media statement afterwards in fact what they believed? If they had laid a complaint with the Department of Nature Conservation against us because they were concerned that Lazarus was too tame for release and had the potential to be dangerous, then what were their plans with Lazzy should he have gone to them?

All these questions floated around in my mind as I tried to make sense of it all. As in any industry, there is the good, the bad, and the ugly side of wildlife conservation. It is here where you need to keep your head up and stay true to your convictions, or else your passion may just be swallowed up by the negativity of it all, as though by a hungry pack of wolves fighting over a bone.

In the end, good came from the complaint that was laid with the Department after all. I was so proud of Lazzy's accomplishments that I wrote to the International Union of Conservation of Nature (IUCN) Species Survival Commission (SSC) Otter Specialist Group. I wanted to share our findings with other like-minded conservationists passionate about the same cause. Far more valuable to us would be to learn from specialised researchers from all parts of the world, and to have access to journal papers on the conservation of the 13 otter species found worldwide. I wrote to the commission, enclosing the same document I had sent to the North West Department of Nature Conservation.

After a few weeks of back-and-forth communication, we were offered full membership of the IUCN/SSC Otter Specialist Group and were "recognized as having made a major and on-going contribution to the conservation of otters." Our work with Lazarus has opened our eyes to the plight of all otters and the effect of human encroachment on their habitat around the world. And our effort to protect them will not end with Lazzy.

Chapter 11

Learning to Fish

I knocked my head on the window as I sat up, startled by a loud groaning noise. It took me a minute or two to gather my thoughts. I was not at home in bed and felt confused by my strange surroundings. In those first few moments after waking, while my brain played catch-up, I had no idea where I was.

We had set up camp once more on the bank of the river, near Lazzy's enclosure, to get an early start in the morning. The day ahead would be an important day in his training and we intended to be up with the lark. At the break of dawn, we planned to take Lazarus to a section of the river where the fish gather in the shallow, slow-flowing parts in the early hours of the day. This would be the opportune time, when fish huddle in the pools, for Lazarus to learn how to catch one.

Rebecca was asleep next to me on the back seat of the Land Rover. The seats recline to nearly flat, and we placed a thin sponge mattress on top of them to make a comfortable bed. Brendan and Spencer were asleep on the roof of the Landy. It was still dark out and impossible to see anything through the windows. They were misted up, covered with condensation, which, aside from the surrounding noises, added to the ghostly feeling and impression of a threatening atmosphere. Deep grunts reverberated in the blackness of the night.

I made a concerted effort not to take any further notice of the sounds floating about in the darkness. Convincing myself that we would be safe inside the vehicle, I managed to calm my nerves enough to go back to sleep. Minutes later, the door opened. It was Spencer. He, too, had heard the loud and oddly eerie noises in an otherwise peaceful atmosphere, and decided to join us inside. He quietly found himself a spot next to Rebecca and within minutes we were all sound asleep again.

In the light of day, we spotted fresh hippo footprints all along the muddy river trail only a few metres from where we had parked. Hippos are considered one of the most dangerous animals on the planet. Not only are they aggressive by nature, they can also be unpredictable. As one of the largest land mammals, no predator would dare take on a beast of this size, and therefore an adult hippo has no natural predator. The male can grow up to 1,800 kg and, if he wanted to, using his lower canine teeth, could chomp right through the tough skin of a crocodile. Crocs have fortunately found a way to co-exist with their moody neighbour and the two animals leave each other in peace.

The idea of a hippo in the nearby vicinity had me more nervous than usual about entering the river. I felt afraid, but this would not deter me from spending time with Lazarus. There was not a day that went by that we were not appreciative of the privilege we had to be working with an otter and to have the opportunity to study him.

I find the process of hands-on research particularly fascinating. This careful observation opens up a window on those small things that we so often overlook. The living world's most extraordinary treasures are discovered when we are willing to take a closer look and open ourselves up to see it from a different perspective and allow that world to flood our mind with new ideas and wonder. When we focus our attention on a particular subject, not only do we learn more about our subject matter but also uncover things about ourselves in the process, it forces us into a deeper level of consciousness about where we fit into it all. Being mindful basically makes us better people.

Researching something means to critically think, evaluate, and study it. In the release project of Lazarus, it meant that I had to fully apply myself to investigate and gain knowledge about the otter species I was working with and where he fitted into his environment. There is a kind of whimsical feeling that awakens within me when I apply this level of awareness to my surroundings. The more I learned about otters through Lazzy, the more I wanted to know about his world, about his wild cousins, and what could be expected of his life in the wild.

Despite all the years that we have worked with owls, I still feel that there is so much more I need to learn. I don't believe the day will ever come when I could say with confidence that I know everything that there is to know about owls, even though I have daily contact with them in many different scenarios. There will always be something more I want to know. I predict that I will probably spend my entire life hungry for knowledge about the animal world, and still, the time I have on this planet will not allow for all the mysteries to be solved and for my mind to feel entirely satisfied.

To fully understand and study animals, especially wildlife, is difficult. It is hard because clear communication between animals and humans is complicated, if not near impossible. What makes research on wild animals even more problematic is the fact that they hardly ever allow us close enough to study them. Wild animals fear people, understandably so, and therefore naturally shy away from us. Under normal conditions, if you were lucky enough to spot an elusive species such as an otter in the wild, a study would for the most part be done from a distance through either binoculars or the lens of a camera. Short glimpses are all you would get.

We had the unique opportunity and honour of learning about Cape clawless otters like few others have ever done. By placing his trust in us, Lazarus allowed us entry into his world. Through our receptivity of Lazzy, his development, behaviour, and his adaptation to a new, natural environment, we learned as and when Lazzy learned. We watched, we observed, and we came to know.

There were no short cuts in the process of helping Lazzy return to the wild. We had to be sure that we were doing what was right for him and that he would be equipped to survive without us when we were no longer around to supervise him and support feed him; to fully understand what his life as a free-living otter in the wild would be like, we had to be willing to become a part of that natural world. We had to, in a way, surrender ourselves to this environment and fully immerse ourselves in it. It would be different from learning about an animal in a zoo or in a controlled research facility where the animal is confined to an abnormal, non-typical habitat. Here, Lazzy could express himself in exactly the same way as an otter living in the wild would.

In return, it was as if a whole new world of balance, harmony, and natural order opened up to us. It is a place where you find the kind of peace within that makes you believe that anything is possible. It took patience and a lot of time, but there are few things in life that I could imagine spending my time on that would provide me with the same amount of gratification. In those moments, it was as if I was in love with life itself.

A quick survey of the area was necessary before we could continue with the planned activities. We would have liked to have access to a drone with the technology of an aerial photography system to do a quick flyover along the river in both directions, to check for crocodile activity or to spot the location of the hippo we now knew was somewhere in the vicinity. Instead, we had to resort to driving along the river, covering kilometers of uneven and slightly mucky ground while scouting for potential danger or risk. Brendan was at the wheel and I had to grab onto whatever grip was available to me, to keep me from landing up on the dashboard of the Land Rover as we bounced up and down, while at the same time using my keen eyesight to scan over the water and banks for animal activity. Brendan found it amusing to terrorise me in the process and would purposely drive fast over bumps to see me bounce high out of my seat. When we assumed it was safe, we went back to fetch Lazarus.

Lazzy was as excited as a child in a chocolate store to be out and about for another day of adventure. The river was delightfully beautiful at this time of the morning. The early-morning rays of light shimmered and danced on the surface of the water. Lazzy was bounding along behind us, his short little legs moving in a jump, leap, dance motion, as we made our way to the dammed-up section of river. In his character, Lazarus reminded me of our golden retriever, Bailey, who is caring, affectionate, true-hearted, and confident. It is no wonder that otters are often referred to as "water dogs." In intelligence, he would put our three border collie pups to shame. (In Bangladesh, otters are trained by fishermen to herd fish into nets, which makes the likeness to collies, who are traditionally trained to herd sheep, quite significant.)

Following our lead, Lazzy ventured into the shallow water at the spot where we had planned to take him fishing. We had done all the necessary preparations for this the day before. By piling sand in a small section on the edge of the river to form a slight barrier wall where the water could pool up, we created a semi-modulated practice area where Lazzy could learn how to catch a fish. As expected, small fish had gathered there to bake in the morning warmth of the sun.

Lazzy noticed the fish the moment he entered the water and instinctively chased after them. He dived in, twisting and turning his body in the water as he tried to get his grip on one. His ability to move around in the fresh river water, which has far less buoyancy than saltwater, in the same way a seal would in the sea, was incredible. He was fit and healthy and his athletic body moved spontaneously in pursuit of his breakfast. My heart felt like it would burst with pride. The same boy who had been afraid of water a little bit more than two months ago had become a skilled swimmer. He was bold and confident as he moved through the water. He was perfectly at home in the wild.

Lazarus as a fisherman was not successful on his first attempt. Nor was he successful on his second, third, or even fourth, but he never lost hope and he kept trying every time with the exact same enthusiasm as the first. We knew that his practice and hard work would pay off in the end, and until then we were there to make sure he had the opportunity to learn. This meant several nights of camping out by the river and early-morning expeditions to where the fish could easiest be caught. The river would wash the sand away that we had piled up to dam the water, and we would have to redo the entire process. In another method, we used a wire cage in which we placed culled day-old chickens, which we buy from a chicken breeder and also use for the owls' diets, and put it in the river to attract catfish that would come to feed on the chickens. This created more opportunity for Lazarus to learn the skill of catching fish.

While he was not successful in those first few attempts, we gave him a fish as reward for his hard work and for the progress he was making. Lazy seemed proud of himself after each attempt, and he carried his fish away with a haughty stride to go wash it in the river and enjoy it somewhere quiet. When he was done, he used his hands to wash his face clean. By and by he would roll around in the river sand, wiggle around in 'S' formations while repeatedly rubbing his paws in smooth motions over his face. Starting from behind his head he would comb with his hands over his eyes and muzzle. This grooming ritual, apart from contributing to his good looks, seemed to soothe him and he would immediately after catch a snooze in the shade of a large tree.

I used this time to set up my "bush office" under a giant white stinkwood tree, semi-sheltered from the scorching heat. I had some catching up to do on e-mails and admin that I had neglected over the weeks and was falling so far behind on that I felt burdened by the workload. The torrid heat around midday made it hard to concentrate. The day temperatures were so intense that the drinking water we had packed felt warm enough to make a cup of coffee or tea.

Before long, Lazzy would become restless again and join Brendan and the kids in the river, where they tried to keep themselves cool in the water. I was sitting quietly, working on my laptop, when Lazarus turned and noticed me sitting on my own. Before long he was by my side, standing up against my leg and moving his wet, sandy little fingers over my keyboard. It was like contending with a naughty preschooler and their soiled little hands. Lazzy was happiest when everyone was together and participating in whatever activity was taking place. I realised quickly that my plan of immersing myself in my work, an activity that did not involve focusing my full attention on Lazzy, was completely futile.

I picked up my camera instead and decided to follow the otter as he explored different areas along the river. He seemed to enjoy this courtesy given to him. It was like he wanted to lead me on an adventure with him. He ran into dense vegetation and then perked up his head, peeking through the greenery to see if I was still there, before carrying on with his expedition, which ended back with Brendan in the river. I watched them playing in the cool waters - Lazzy, Brendan, and the kids - and thought that this must be the epitome of happiness.

One day our children will look back on these moments and realise how incredibly lucky they were. I hope that in that future world there is still the possibility for these kinds of experiences. I hope that otters will still be around, rivers will be clean enough to swim in, and people will still have the kind of spiritual connection with Nature to appreciate our natural world.

A Healthy Appetite

By Brendan Murray

We never weighed Lazzy but I did carry him around quite a bit during playtime. If I had to guess, I would say he was around 10 kg, which is relatively small for a male of his species. But when it came to eating, he would easily put a 1-kg fish away in around eight minutes. That coupled with all the freshwater mussels and crabs that he foraged and ate meant he would consume around 15% of his own body weight on a good day.

Danelle with Lazzy.

Lazzy peaks into the Land Rover to see what fish we brought him.

Lazzy washes his fish in the river.

Lazzy rips pieces of a catfish as he eats.

The fish is almost the same size as Lazzy.

Chapter 12

Nature's Child

Our kids were born into a life of conservation. Ever since they were old enough to understand, their entire world has been about caring for and protecting animals. They have grown up amongst the owls and other wildlife that have, since their earliest memories, filled our home. There are also the several rescued, adopted pets that are an important part of our family dynamic. Spencer and Rebecca were both very little still when they started helping us, where they could, by feeding or pitching in with the husbandry requirements of these animals. I often wonder if they appreciate the privilege of a life shared with so many fascinating creatures. For them, it is the norm and there is no other kind of life. Even if they do not realise it now, the interactions they share with these beings will come to serve them well in later years. These animals have an influence over their lives, far greater than may be understood right now.

The importance of allowing undomesticated animals to return to the wild is a principle that has been instilled in them from the start. As much as their love and affection for Lazarus grew in the time we spent with him, they wanted Lazzy to be free to live the life he was meant to as much as Brendan and I did. I was proud to know we had kids that could be selfless enough to place the needs of an animal before their own need to want to hold onto him. This is probably the biggest and most important lesson that we learn in working with animals: to be selfless.

Spencer and Rebecca are both keen readers of nature books, most of which have been donated to us over the years (enough to fill a small library), and have accumulated a wealth of knowledge about animals from across the globe. Rebecca speaks about becoming a vet one day, while Spencer dreams of living in the Amazon rainforest, protecting endangered animals like hyacinth macaws, white-cheeked spider monkeys, jaguars, and even the giant otter. From the age of nine, Spencer joined us on regular hiking expeditions, five-hour strenuous walks on harsh terrain made up of rocks, riverine, uneven ground of ravine and gorges, blazing hot sand, and grassland.

We hiked up the Magaliesberg mountain not only for the beautiful surroundings that enveloped you on the way up, but for the ultimate reward of observing a colony of about 600 Cape vultures who nest on the cliffs of the mountainside. We would hike up to the peak to a spot on the left of the nesting area, from where we would have a clear view looking down onto the colony without causing any disturbance to them. Some vultures would take off and soar out in front of us, floating effortlessly through the boundless blue sky. Some would turn back over the mountain and overhead where we sat, so near to us that we could see the finest detail of their feathers and look straight into their gazing eyes. They would curiously turn their heads at an angle to glare down at us, almost as if pausing to see what kind of animals we were.

What was notable about these hikes that Spencer accompanied us on wasn't the fact that a child of his age could ably climb the mountain to its very top, often leading the group at the front, but rather that he did this entire trek barefoot. So comfortable was he in this environment that he navigated it unshod. His feet had grown strong to tolerate the topography they were exposed to daily, and he walked the landscape effortlessly shoeless.

Spencer and Rebecca both refused to wear shoes when they were little. Try as I might, by buying the most comfortable shoes I could find, they protested every time I wanted them to wear shoes. For my children, it was the most natural thing in the world to be barefoot. In fact, it's ironic just how "unnatural" it has become for people to go barefoot nowadays. I used to force both kids to wear shoes whenever we went out to public places or to visit friends and family, to avoid the inevitable line of questioning I soon came to expect, accompanied by the look that suggested I was somehow failing as a mother: "Don't they have shoes?," or "Aren't their feet cold?," or the just plain "Where are their shoes?"

Rebecca would make it as far as the car before pulling them off and tossing them like trash she was happy to be rid of. "My feet want to be free, Mommy!" she would say, "They don't like to be caged."

They were and still are children of the bare earth. Whether they will realise their dreams and continue in this life of conservation, only time will tell. They are under no illusion about how hard it can be at times. They are both still very young and there will be plenty of time for them to make up their minds about their future.

Watching Lazzy gain competence within his environment was something that, for me as a mother, carried sentiment. I realised that, like Lazarus, one day the time will come for my own children to find their place in the world. Every day we spend with them, we facilitate this process of growth and development of qualities that will help them some day to cope in this world without us. It is for this reason - understanding the importance of environmental influences and stimuli - that we decided to home-school our children and not educate them through the conventional schooling system. Apart from our lifestyle requirements of spending time in remote areas, we wanted them to grow up with traditional values - values from a time before technology and modern society took over the evolution of the youth and our future generations.

Brendan and I both feel that there is a large part missing from the lives of young people today. Spencer and Rebecca are growing up without access to cell phones and other devices that we feel are unnecessary accessories at their age. Without the usual peer pressure children experience at school, this has never been an issue for them. Instead, they are encouraged to read books, explore the living world, and learn through regular play. I spent most of my childhood outside in the fresh open air, building little houses made from sticks, leaves. and stones, dancing in the long grass and allowing my imagination to soar free. What better teacher is there than Nature to teach creativity, purpose, balance, survival, understanding, respect, and responsibility?

Instead, today's children spend a large portion of their lives learning from and living in the artificial world of the internet. I believe that much of the trouble with the world today can be explained by this, but this is not the book for that debate! My concern, however, is with the growing gap that exists between humans and nature. Unless we close this gap, the future of conservation seems bleak.

Back in 2014, when we acquired the farm now known as the Owl Sanctuary, we were realising our dream to secure a piece of protected habitat that would always belong to the owls. It would be a place where owls can be cared for and released within a safe environment. The farm is a 45-ha piece of land that falls within a larger protected area within the Magaliesberg Conservancy. It rests at the foot of the Magalies mountain range and is the ideal habitat for owls.

We did not have the funding to buy the property and despite several efforts to obtain a loan, we were turned down by the bank each and every time. We needed to put down at least 50% of the total purchase price before the bank would consider giving us a loan. For them, there was far too much risk in giving a bond for a property of this size to a non-profit organisation. When we couldn't arrange a loan but were determined to see our plan through, we met with the owner and negotiated a Deed of Sale agreement in which we pay for the property in instalments paid directly to him. As luck would have it, he was desperate to sell and wanted to move down to the coast, so he agreed to our terms.

Apart from the topography being perfect for owls, the property came with a very run-down and rustic lodge consisting of a few chalets, a bush camp, and tented accommodation. This, we thought, was how we could generate the funds to cover the costs of the property and to pay for the rescue and rehabilitation bills we accumulated each month. Our initial idea was to invite like-minded people who care about nature and conservation to sign up as members of the organisation. As an incentive to become involved and pay the membership fee, we would offer them each a two-day accommodation package to stay over in the lodge. This meant that members would be able to see first-hand what our projects are about, and we were excited to have families stay over and reconnect with the bush in the basic and unfettered way in which we get to experience it every day.

We jumped right in and got the place fixed up. We worked day and night. We varnished, painted, repaired, and redecorated the whole place, working our fingers to the bone to realise our dream. It was a bushveld paradise when we were done. But try as we might, we couldn't get enough people to sign up for our membership programme - not enough anyway to cover the huge monthly bond that we had to pay to stick to our agreement with the owner of the property. With no other options available to us, we decided against our better judgement to open the lodge to the public. It was December of that same year, the major holiday season, that we officially opened our doors as Morubisi Bush Lodge - *morubisi* meaning "owl" in Setswana, the native language of the area, felt like the appropriate name to give it.

I remember how excited we were to share our piece of paradise with other people. Little did we know what we were getting ourselves into. It was no longer only conservation-conscious people who would come and spend a night out in the bush, but anyone looking for a break from the city or an escape from home. Sometimes, it was just people looking for a place where they could meet up with friends to party. More often than not, these people had no interest in the spectacular setting or the work that we were doing, but had booked with us purely because we offered inexpensive accommodation.

As much as I loathed those years of running the lodge, it did teach me, with significant first-hand insight, about the need for wildlife conservation education. I realised during that time (which lasted no longer than three years before we made the decision to close it for good), how little tolerance people have left for wildlife and nature, and how much they have forgotten to appreciate the natural world around them. Guests complained about so many things that I wondered why they would even consider booking a place that had the word "bush lodge" in its name: "There are too many frogs; they are croaking too loud." "The owls kept us up all night with their constant hooting." "A zebra stole my sandwich that I left on the table outside my tent." And so on and so on.

Once, a family with kids, two boys similar in age to our own children, booked with us. I always got excited when families with young children booked because I knew that it was a great place for them and always thought that kids, at least, still got excited by the countryside, even if their parents didn't. Spencer and Rebecca were thrilled for the opportunity to show them around. First on the agenda was to show them what they referred to as the Magic Tree.

The Magic Tree is a giant wild olive that grows at the top-most part of our property, right where the landscape dips into a valley and the ravine that runs along the base of the mountain. It is magnificent, tall, and wondrous. With the wisdom of a life lived over a few hundred years, our kids came to the conclusion that there must be a magical element to such an enduring earthly being. Their imaginations created a make-believe story about the tree. In their fantasy world, you could ask this tree questions to which it would give you the answers, but only within your mind's eye. "When you are really quiet, you can hear her whisper the answer inside your head," they would tell me. I played along and listened attentively to all the stories they told about their cherished tree.

Their young guests, who they had eagerly shared this secret sacred information with, showed no interest in the tree at all.

"What are we doing at a stupid tree?" the one exclaimed.

"Can we go watch TV now?" the other echoed.

Later that day, their mother approached me to ask if my kids might have PlayStation for the children so that they could entertain themselves. "They are terribly bored," she added.

"No sorry, they don't," I replied, without going into detail about our take on TV and computer games and their negative effects on children.

"Oh shame!" she said in a condescending tone. She must have thought that we were too poor to buy our children such toys.

I stood baffled by her reaction for a minute or so, and then I just smiled. For me, there was a great deal of irony in her perception, for it was her own two children that I pitied instead. How much they would miss out on in this life, living and growing only between the constricts of walls, absent-mindedly staring in front of them like zombies at a screen. We live in a new type of world, where there is so little potential for the imagination to roam free, so little appreciation for the simple things that are rudimentary to living a happy and wholesome life. I shudder to think what will happen to our planet if all our youth had to become that disinterested in nature...

The divide between humans and nature becomes greater with every new wall that is built. Every new building, housing complex, or shopping mall that goes up pushes nature further and further away from us. One day we will live in a world where all the space has been taken up, and animals like Lazarus will no longer have a place in it. Many will mock the "tree-hugging" activists for fighting to preserve a wetland or preventing a development from going ahead, but fail to understand the effect of these subtle changes that are gradually taking place all around us. If we do not fight for what is left now, in the end there will be nothing left to fight for.

I believe that the human-animal relationship and our connection to nature is the key to a healthier and better world. Maybe if the benefits we gain from animals and nature were better understood by all, people would be more inclined to protect and hold on to what we have? Animals teach us qualities of kindness, tolerance, patience, adaptability, responsibility, harmony, and order. Animals and nature have the power to heal us and to reduce our stress; they provide companionship to the lonely and the depressed, and can help us through life's difficulties.

It is sad, then, that so many children grow up without any contact with animals, especially in African countries where poverty prevails. Having a pet is a luxury many cannot afford. When you battle to provide for your own basic needs, taking care of the needs of another life, a non-human life at that, is out of the question. My children are being raised to protect and conserve the animals that are a part of their realm, while other children are preoccupied by the merciless effects of poverty. Many of these kids grow up never knowing the joy an animal can provide, never understanding the bond that can develop between a person and an animal, and never feeling the emotional connectedness that exists in a human-animal relationship. Can we then expect a child who has never experienced this to have enough appreciation of animals in the wild to feel driven to protect them?

Poverty also results in the over-use of natural resources in an unsustainable way, such as hunting certain species to the point of extinction. Our task as conservationists is far-reaching. It goes beyond the rescue and care of a single animal, or even a species; it goes beyond teaching our own children the importance of caring for the environment; it even goes beyond the fancy scientific studies that provide us with insight about animals and the environment. Unless we are able to solve some of the social problems and bridge the gap between nature and the children of today, our efforts are nothing more but futile hope.

Chapter 13

Big Snake

In the nineteenth century. otters were hunted to near extinction. Their beautiful, warm and luxurious pelts, thick with 100,000 hairs per cm^2, were much sought-after and resulted in indiscriminate hunting for what was one of the most highly prized animal furs at the time. The hunters familiarised themselves with the otters' habits, such as secreting a scent at specific locations to mark out their territory, which made it easy for them to track the otters for the kill. This drastically reduced population numbers in some areas to a mere 1% of what it used to be.

Fortunately, biologists and conservationists realised the otter's importance in the ecosystem and regulations were put in place to protect them. The otter population managed to make a recovery in most parts of the world, but still to this day all 13 otter species are considered vulnerable, with the likelihood of extinction. This is a bitter pill to swallow when you have had the pleasure of meeting a fellow like Lazarus. Otters are fun-loving, communicative, inquisitive, intelligent, unassuming beings. These are all characteristics that the best among humans constantly strive to embody. Even so, otters are mindlessly threatened by mankind. In all parts of the world, the survival of otter species and their future on our planet are hanging in the balance.

Despite the protection regulations, there are still parts of the world where otters are hunted for their fur as well as for their bones. These products are exported to places like India and China where they are used in traditional medicine. The illegal wildlife trade is a huge concern for the protection of most species and carries, according to the United Nations Environmental Program (UNEP), a market value of approximately 200 billion dollars. The power that lies behind such an amount of money is hard to contend with. In places like Bangladesh, where otters were prominent inhabitants of wetlands, they have become near extinct.

Conservation efforts are often focused on preventing the illegal wildlife trade and protection of larger animals such as elephants, lions, leopards, and rhinos. Very little attention is given to smaller animals like otters. To make matters worse, otters face many more threats besides the ruthless wildlife trade industry. In underdeveloped countries, otters are blamed by fishermen for competing for food and are trapped and then often killed. Fish farms view them as problematic animals who steal their stock, even though most otters prefer molluscs over fish as a snack. In some cases, they are hunted as food themselves. What is more, otters are running out of natural habitat and good, pollution-free places to live. Therefore, finding a suitable release spot for a hand-reared otter like Lazarus is not an easy undertaking, and careful consideration is required to find a suitable spot unaffected by contamination and human encroachment. We had to consider the water quality, food availability (which usually goes hand in hand with water quality), the surrounding area, and distance from human settlements.

In less developed countries, people often settle and build villages near to rivers and streams. The villagers then wash their clothing in this nearby water. The detergents contaminate and pollute the water, which results in an ecological imbalance and poor water quality. It is also the careless management of waste, including in developed countries, that is affecting the water quality of rivers all around the world. This waste and pollution bring about disease and an entire disturbance of the ecological equilibrium. Otters have a low tolerance for pollutants and are considered to be bio-indicators of poor water quality. The absence of otters in an area helps scientists to realise that there may be high levels of pollutants in the water.

In 1969, zoologist Robert T. Paine coined a phrase for animals which have an exceptionally large effect on their natural environment in relation to their size and population. He called these animals "keystone" species. The term "keystone" is best explained in the construction of an arch. The stone at the top centre of an arch holds the entire structure in place. If the central keystone of an arch is removed, all the other stones come tumbling down. In the same way, removing a certain animal or plant from an environment results in an ecological phenomenon known as a trophic cascade. It is a simple cause-and-effect scenario in which one small action can result in a drastic change.

Sea otters are one of those special animals that holds the important title of keystone species. They mainly feed on sea urchins, which are grazers of kelp. By this predation, the sea urchin population is controlled and relieves their feeding demand on the kelp, which allows kelp forests to flourish. Nature is in perfect balance if left undisturbed by human interference.

With so many factors against a species, including conflict with humans and hunters, ecological disturbances and loss of habitat, it is surprising then that otters still occur in almost every part of the world (with the exception of Antarctica and Oceania) and, amazingly, not one of the 13 species of otters has become extinct yet. From my observations of Lazarus, their intelligence, flexibility, and zest for life have certainly contributed to their survival.

In one of our many research projects, we covered a very remote and almost undiscovered part of South Africa in search of otters, to measure their occurrence and population. Our travels started on the West Coast of the country and brought us to the outlying Richtersveld National Park, which runs along the border between South Africa and Namibia. The area is a Ramsar site, a wetland of international importance, because of its richness of biodiversity. Although undeniably beautiful, it is bone dry and deserted. We drove hundreds of kilometres through the unspoilt and silent landscape. One day, after travelling for about 10 hours straight along a rough, rutted dirt road that runs along the beach, known as the Wildeperdhoek Pass, from where we had a perfect unspoiled view of the rocks, landscape, and seashore to scout for wildlife, we reached a small village in the Namakwa district known as Hondeklipbaai (roughly translated from Afrikaans as Dog Rock Bay). It is home to mainly subsistence fishermen and diamond miners.

Apart from them, the village was packed with tourists from all over the world, which were most likely, like us, attracted to its remoteness. The fact that the village is largely inaccessible to most travellers is what gives it its unique charm, and, ironically, makes people want to flock there to experience its simple, unassuming allure. The village seemed almost entirely unaffected by the modern world, its cultural heritage remained mostly unchanged and preserved through the decades. It is like time stood still here. No construction or development were taking place, only a repetition of the same day-to-day activities of fishing, mining, eating, drinking, entertaining, and partying. The people still live close to the earth. The houses are informal, small, and modest. The roads are wide and plain gravel.

As we arrived, we were received with the warmest hospitality I have ever experienced. The locals are unpretentious and seem high on life itself. Every person we came across greeted us with a warm and friendly smile. Dessie, an outgoing, cordial woman in her thirties, welcomed us at an accommodation spot in the hub of the village.

"My goodness but you have travelled far," she said.

As I climbed out of the car, my legs felt like jelly after sitting for such a long time. It was starting to get dark outside and it had felt like the road to the town was never-ending. It felt good to be greeted with such pure friendliness. I had explained the purpose of our trip and she seemed genuinely interested to know more about our project.

"Wait, I need to introduce you to some people."

She called whoever was within earshot to tell them about our work. Then she hopped into the Land Rover to direct us to the tented camp where we would be staying the night. There we were introduced to more people who grew up in the area. And just like that, Dessie was our personal tour advisor who introduced us to several residents of Hondeklip Bay, which helped us in our research. We were able to interview several people about otter sightings in the area. Dessie wished us a good night before leaving for home and hugged me goodbye like she had known me for years. In this little town, people are never strangers for long.

We left early the next morning and made it to Alexandria Bay by midday. From here, there were very few distinguishable roads and we drove along a dry riverbed to our next destination, where we were to set up camp on the banks of the Orange River. The wetlands that were once here have been disturbed by the diamond mining and poor management of natural resources in the area. The mining practices have restricted natural water flow in the interior habitat, which threatens the many species dependent on it, including several endangered waterbird species, reptile species, and mammal species.

Years ago, a large population of Cape clawless otters were in the area, so much so that a legend arose among the local people of a "big snake" who roamed in the wetlands. It was later discovered that the "big snake" was in fact the rippling effect of the Cape clawless otter's swimming, moving its thick long tail in slithering motions through the surface of the water. To our dismay, we could not find any sign of an otter anywhere in the area. No one we spoke to had seen an otter in the last couple of years. Sadly, the impact of our actions on the environment is often realised when it is almost too late. Our immediate needs supersede our responsibility to protect the Earth for those who come after us.

When it comes to matters of conservation, I came to the realisation many years ago that there are, generally speaking, two types of people in this world. There are those who appreciate everything around them simply for what it is. They are supportive and grateful for the people in their lives. They enthusiastically encourage wildlife to visit their gardens. They cherish the natural environment around them - the life in the trees, the sound of the birds, the wind and smell in the air when they are out for a walk. Then there are those who appreciate only what is of direct benefit to them. This kind of person values people who can advance them in life and does not burn energy on those who cannot. They appreciate animals only in relation to themselves and what they can get out of having animals around them, whether it be comfort, entertainment or amusement, protection, money, or other functions animals fulfil. The environment they live in should function to suit their personal needs. This is the person who complains about the mess birds make on the pavement, the hooting owl that disturbs their sleep, the impudent audacity of the little lizard who enters their bathroom through an open window ... For them, animals have a right to live only when their existence has some direct benefit to them.

We get to deal with both these kinds of people on a regular basis. We once received a call from a lady who insisted that we come and capture the barn owls who live in a palm tree in her garden.

"Why would you want us to move them somewhere else," I asked, "when they have chosen to live there?"

"They make a mess on the lawn," she said. "What if my kids pick up the pellets? It is unsanitary."

Instead of teaching her kids not to pick up the owl pellets, she expected us to catch and relocate perfectly healthy owls. The problem is, we as humans have inhabited most of the space left for these animals. If this becomes the general mindset, where do we relocate these owls?

The first kind are natural conservationists who believe in the preservation of not just nature but beauty, history, life, and heritage. They want this not only for themselves to treasure, but also for those who will live many years after them. They appreciate beings purely for being. The latter kind are the ones who need a bit more convincing to motivate them to protect other life forms. They will love the tree in their garden that provides them with shade, but cut down the tree that drops its leaves in winter. They will go on holiday in reserves for game drives to view the wildlife that are fascinating to observe, but kill the wildlife who chew up their vegetable garden.

These people often make me want to jump on my soapbox and proclaim to them what thoughtless standards they live by. I want to shake them to wake them up to a deeper understanding of life in an interconnected system. But before I express my "prejudiced"opinion to the person who tells me that owls do not belong in areas where humans live, I remind myself that people reflect their own life experiences in their attitude to the world. Their interactions with people, animals, and other stimuli have shaped their mindset. Their upbringing, education, customs, practices, and experiences with both people and the natural world, all contributed to this response.

Very often, people express their own pain through their intolerance of other living things. If I were to have any value in the work that I do, it would be to use the advantage I have of daily experiences with animals and nature to educate and teach those who are not as fortunate and blessed as I am. Maybe someday this will translate into an all-encompassing collaboration to protect our planet.

Chapter 14

Water Dog

Lazzy wiggled himself a cosy spot in the sand, looking up at me with his puppy-dog eyes. They were dark cocoa-coloured brown, and looked like the fabric-covered buttons on a coat. His pelt was smooth and shiny and reflected the sunlight. It no longer had the knots and matted appearance of when he first came to us. The day's activities had eventually worn down the fleet-footed otter, who just minutes ago had chased after Brendan in the shallow water in what seemed like a game of touch or fartlek (named for the Swedish word for "fast run") and play-biting. He capered around in the water, splashing as he ran after Brendan. He squeaked and groaned with excitement each time he succeeded in his race to catch up to Brendan.

When he did, Brendan stood hunched over him and Lazzy rolled over onto his back, grasping Brendan's calf in his hands and lightly placing his mouth around his ankles. His long, sharp teeth softly clasped Brendan's ankle bone. The playful mouthing, which appeared to be the objective of the chase, was gentle and affectionate. There was not a hint of aggression in his behaviour. At this, Brendan would tease him and tickle his tummy. Lazzy would respond with short growls, grabbing at Brendan's hands like a baby snatching at a toy. Then he would dart off excitedly into the water, running, splashing and sprinting in a wide circle, before returning to play the same game all over again.

While acting playful, he made a melodic sound much like the famous tauntauns, the snow lizards of Hoth in the popular *Star Wars* films. Lazzy would express his feelings through sounds, which over time we got to know the meaning of. These different vocal expressions varied from high-pitched whistling to chirps, groans, and grunts. It was like a language of its own. Without words, Lazarus spoke to us. He could not, however, communicate to me the exact meaning behind the look in his eyes as he lay there gazing up at me with tenderness. I was almost sure that he was trying to tell me something far more complex than what his usual verbal expressions could allow for. Maybe it was that he knew instinctively that things would not always be this way - that a day would come when he would have to go out on his own and live and play among his own kind.

I myself was grappling with this reality, and maybe it was my own emotion that was projected through his eyes. It had over time become easier to part with an owl when the time came for it to be released, but this situation, working with an otter like Lazzy, somehow seemed hugely different. Over the years, various owls have touched our hearts and we have many treasured memories of time spent with them, but birds capture your affection in a different way than mammals. Besides, we put systems in place when rehabilitating the owls to make sure that our contact with and impact on them are minimal. Owls do not require the kind of personal attention from us in the way that Lazzy did, and owls hardly express emotion as he did. Lazzy displayed his feelings all over his face.

Baby owls are hand-reared only for a few weeks before they are handed to a foster mommy owl to take over the responsibility of their feeding and care. We discovered their tendency to adopt another's offspring by pure accident when we placed a young spotted eagle owl with an adult female in an overnight enclosure. She forthwith took the youngster under her wing and later started tearing pieces of meat from a rat we had provided to feed the baby. Our foster adoption programme is extremely successful and ensures that the owlets do not imprint on us in any way. This is, of course, vital for their survival and future in the wild.

We have a few owls at the Sanctuary that are not candidates for release because they have sustained irreparable damage through injury. Some have wing injuries and would not be able to hunt for themselves; others are almost completely blind. They have a good life in a huge habitat aviary, an enclosure that closely mimics their natural terrain, constructed around large trees in which they can move around freely but in a controlled environment where food is provided. These owls have the important function as our surrogate moms who raise rescued and orphaned owlets. Their innate motherly instincts kick in with the first feeding call of a baby and they, without any hesitation, adopt the stranded youngster. The babies grow and develop naturally under the watchful care of the surrogate mom, and leave the aviary at the same time a juvenile owl in the wild would leave its parents to find its own territory.

We had even introduced rescued owlets to free-living owls that were not in a restricted environment, such as an enclosure where the adults are directly confronted by the baby, but simply within the pair's breeding territory. This has also been successful on several occasions, especially with breeding pairs who had offspring of their own. The adopted baby is treated equally to the owl pair's own young, enjoying the same protection, care, and patience shown to their biological brood. Handing them over in this relatively early stage of their growth process makes it easier to part with them, and there is less chance of a sentimental attachment arising from contact with them.

But with Lazarus, without any deliberate intention, we developed a deep emotional connection as he thrived under our constant care and attention. He felt like an extension of our family, much like our family dogs. A kindred relationship manifests between a human and an animal capable of this level of cognitive ability. There is much speculation about intelligence, emotional capacity, and even emotional awareness in animals. Many sceptics would roll their eyes at me if they heard me explain the thought processes I had observed in Lazzy, and accuse me of anthropomorphising - attributing human behaviour and characteristics, such as the ability to experience emotion in the same way as we do, to an animal. Some scientists would argue that the reactions we observed were purely reactive mechanisms to either environmental threats or to reward. I would counter-argue this every time. I think we give animals far too little credit.

Take, for example, the fascinating story of Jack the baboon. Back in 1881 a chacma baboon was trained by a railway signalman, James Wide, who had lost both his legs in an accident, to act as his assistant. Jack pushed him around on a cart James had built for himself, and under James's supervision the animal helped him to operate the railway signals. It is said that James first met Jack at a marketplace in Uitenhage, near Port Elizabeth, where he saw him leading an ox wagon. Astounded by the baboon's intelligence and skill, and realising how an animal like Jack could help him in his own daily struggles, he implored Jack's owner to sell him the baboon. The man, who felt sorry for James, agreed. James moved Jack into his small cottage near the railway line and the two would set off to work together every morning. Jack would push James in the cart on the uphill section, and would jump into the cart with him for the downhill ride to the station.

Believe it or not, the story does not end there. Jack soon became proficient enough in signalling that he no longer needed to take instruction from James. He could operate the railway signs by pulling on levers, which would give the order to the railway engineers of which track they must take, entirely on his own. It was only when a notable member of the public spotted Jack at Uitenhage Station operating the railway signals, and expressed her concern and outrage over a primate managing this important function, that an investigation was undertaken by the railway authorities. After much scepticism, as one could imagine, and conducting several tests to showcase his abilities, Jack was officially employed by the railway services at Uitenhage Station. He worked there for nine years, earning 20 cents a day and half a bottle of beer a week. He operated the railway signals until his death in 1890, when he succumbed to tuberculosis. It is said that he never, in his entire nine years of service, made a single mistake.

If there were ever an animal to prove to me the presence of both emotion and intelligence, it was Lazarus. Although we would only recognize his actual brilliance a bit later in the process, he had already demonstrated efficiency in his environment beyond anyone's expectations. He had gone from an animal raised by humans in a confined space to a fully functional aquatic animal. An otter once afraid of water, now manoeuvred through the river with superior skill. I have watched as he expressed fear, doubt, amusement, boredom, fondness, desire, disappointment, sadness, and many other human-like emotions throughout his journey of discovery.

Through him I was reminded that neither our minds nor our bodies are static, and we can develop and adapt to whatever we need to to further ourselves in life if we are only willing to try. Lazzy reminds us of our ability to learn new skills, even if we think that it may be too late. I have observed him closely to try to identify the resentment he must have felt for being kept from the life he deserved for all those years, but this was never expressed in his actions. He lived only in the here and now. He never wallowed in the past. Freedom became his only desire, and any time before the present no longer had any relevance to him.

The more Lazzy learned and developed, the closer the time came for his release. We would not hold him back longer than necessary. He was nearly ready, and we would soon have to let him go out in the wild without our supervision or our protection. It was exciting to see these changes in him and to know that he was almost ready to live his life in the wild. At the same time, it was sad to know that our time with him, these merry moments in paradise, was running out. During this precious time, he felt like a natural part of our lives, but we could not ignore that the day was dawning to let him go. Saying our final goodbyes would be a bittersweet affair. Although we knew from the start that Lazzy would return to the wild in the end, it still felt as if we were going to leave one of our pups out there in the wilderness. Fortunately, clever as he was, Lazarus would find a way to make this transition easier on us.

As the sun was about to set and the sky filled with the brightest shades of orange, red, and magenta, we gathered up some dry driftwood and Brendan made a fire on the river sand for us to cook on. In a black cast-iron pot, we made a stew with vegetables and I opened a bottle of red wine and poured us each a glass to enjoy with sundown. I sniffed into the glass to take in the earthy aroma. In that moment, I felt as if I was exactly where I was supposed to be. I had no longing for anything more. This was exactly what I had imagined, all those years ago, when I thought about what my life would be like working with wildlife. I had wanted nothing more than to experience what it would be like to live in the open wilderness, free as the animals themselves, and passionately striving to make a valuable difference in the lives of those who couldn't do it for themselves.

It has not always worked out to be the perfect life, and not all of the expectations of the job make it feel like a charmed career. Heartache, frustration, and feelings of hopelessness are undeniable when working with animals. But it is those despairing periods that make me cherish moments such as these, under the stars in the wild, that much more. If I had to die tomorrow, I would do so knowing that my life had been meaningful.

Adopting Lazzy

By Brendan Murray

I often think back to the day Lazarus was dropped off and introduced to Danelle and me. It felt almost the same as adopting a foster child of the same age. A four-year-old otter is playful, adventurous, curious, demanding, and full of mixed emotions, much the same as a human child. And as with adopting a human child, this little dude came with a fair amount of stress.

He isn't like any of the other wildlife we have rehabilitated and released; owls come in, we medicate them, bandage them, feed them, and, when healed, they go into a pre-release enclosure. Once they are flying fit, they are free to go back to the wild. It is a relatively easy process whereby you hardly get attached to the patient.

Six months, averaging six hours spent with Lazzy almost every day, he became your child. The fear I had of something bad happening to the little monster is inexplicably high. It is an irrational fear.

Lazzy peaks out from the thick green vegetation that grows along the river

Danelle observes Lazzy eating a catfish.

Lazzy returns from a swim in the river.

Lazzy play bites Danelle's hand.

Chapter 15

Breaking Free

Over the next few days, we were busy as beavers with rescues and owl releases. We had taken in hundreds of owls over winter. They had gone through their rehabilitation and were all ready to return to the wild. Because of the warmer temperatures and higher food availability, springtime is the most favourable time of the year for animals in the wild, and therefore our releases are planned around this. Apart from Lazzy's, we were managing two other release sites: one for barn owls and another for southern white-faced owls.

The two release sites were both in the Madikwe Game Reserve on the border of Botswana, but at opposite ends of the vast property. They both required monitoring to ensure that the releases are successful. In each case, a "soft-release" process was followed to help with the gradual adaptation to a new environment. Every minute of every day was accounted for - monitoring, checking, and taking food supplies to each site. It was the remoteness of these sites that made it a particularly laborious undertaking. We worked day and night, seven days a week. This also meant that we had less time to spend with Lazarus. Our usual four- to six-hour sessions with him were reduced to as little as an hour a day on some days.

When we could not be there, Godfrey ensured that Lazzy was happy and healthy and that his living standards were top-notch. Every morning he would drive the tractor with the water-tank trailer down to the enclosure. He would use a big, long flexible water pipe to syphon the old water from Lazzy's water bath into the river, clean the bath out, and then fill it with fresh water. The stench that accumulated from the bits and pieces of fish from Lazzy washing his food in this water, a 500-L water trough, was unbelievable. There was no way that it could be left for longer than a day without being cleaned.

One morning at around 7:00 a.m., on one of these routine trips, Godfrey was surprised to find Lazzy's enclosure empty when he got there. The gate was locked as normal, the latch securely in place, but there was no sign of the expected friendly face that greeted him every other morning when he arrived at the enclosure. Baffled, he unfastened the lock and climbed inside to check the wooden house, to see if Lazzy had decided to sleep in for a bit. Fears that the otter might be ill filled his head. But after checking the entire enclosure and every possible hiding spot, Lazzy was nowhere to be seen. It was as if he had vanished into thin air.

Godfrey phoned Brendan to check whether we may have arrived earlier that morning to take Lazzy on a walk and for a swim further down the river, without his knowledge.

"Are you on the farm?" he asked, ignoring all the usual greeting formalities.

"Howzit, Godfrey. No, we can only get out there a bit later, mid-morning or so." Brendan balanced the phone with his shoulder, pressing it to his ear.

"Lazzy's gone. I can't find him anywhere."

There was silence on both ends of the phone. Carefully studying Brendan's face, while holding a barn owl in position for him to continue to strap its broken wing, I could see the colour drain from his face. I could tell that something was wrong.

"What do you mean gone?"

"He was not in his enclosure this morning. I can't find him anywhere."

I told Brendan that I would finish up on my own in the clinic. "You better go see where he is," I said with a heaviness in my heart.

Without a second thought, Brendan left everything exactly as it was and rushed out to the release farm. All manner of fears entered our minds. He promised to call me the minute he had news.

When he arrived, he double-checked the enclosure, hoping that Godfrey had somehow missed Lazzy hiding away somewhere. However unlikely this may have seemed, the idea of him missing without a trace was even more inconceivable. But just as Godfrey had said, Lazarus was nowhere to be seen. There were no holes anywhere along the border of the enclosure where he could have dug his way out. Godfrey had said with certainty that the gate of the enclosure was securely closed upon his arrival. So how was it then that Lazzy was missing from it?

Our only conclusion could be that Godfrey must have accidentally let him out and lost track of the little otter as he went on one of his expeditions along the riverbed.

"Maybe he is afraid to tell us that he made an honest mistake," I said when Brendan phoned me to confirm Lazzy's mysterious disappearance.

But Godfrey is an honest man who does admit when he has made a blunder, so that notion was ruled out almost immediately after we had voiced it.

Brendan left food for Lazarus inside his enclosure in case he returned hungry. Then he set off looking for him. We knew Lazzy well enough to know that he would not head to the northern side of the farm, away from the river into bushveld terrain. Like any other otter, he wanted to be along the river. This was where he felt at home. There were too many spoors left over from his excursions of the days before to follow a track in the direction he had most likely gone. Did he follow the river downstream or did he go in the opposite direction?

Brendan started his search as far upstream as he could get, following the river for kilometres down, exploring all Lazzy's usual favourite spots along the way. The vegetation was too dense in areas right beside the river to walk there, and the embankment too steep or too high to get a proper view of the water, which made it unworkable to explore the area on land. This meant that Brendan had to get in the water and wade around in the river in the hope of spotting the little otter. "Lazzy, Lazzy my boy!" he called out as he made his way along currents of flowing water.

I waited anxiously for an update, but hours passed before Brendan phoned. My stomach was in a knot and the worry hung over me like a dark cloud for the entire day. I felt ill. The thought that something terrible could have happened to Lazzy preyed on my mind.

Brendan spent more than eight hours in the river under the scorching sun, which reached temperatures of over 40°C. I could hear the weariness in his voice when he broke the news. There was still no sign of our beloved otter. Brendan was red as a lobster from the sunburn. His feet were cut up by sharp rocks and mussel shells from walking along the rough, shallow sections of the riverbed. With daylight fading into darkness, Brendan had no option but to put off his search until the next morning. He agreed to come home and the two of us planned to return before sunrise the next day to carry on searching the area. He had hardly left the farm when his phone rang. It was Godfrey.

"I have good news! He is here. I found Lazzy!" he said. "I was so happy to see him, I felt like I wanted to hug him."

It turned out that Lazzy had had the time of his life that day. Godfrey found him playing on the sandbank near the river crossing, a low concrete overpass that connects the northern part of the farm to the more mountainous section. He was frolicking near the water when Godfrey spotted him. When Godfrey called him, he just turned and looked at him as if to say, "Oh, there you are!" and then followed him back to the enclosure. His belly was pudgy and round; so much so that he showed no interest in the food that Godfrey supplied for dinner. It was clear that he now knew how to feed himself.

Chapter 16
Lazzy the Illusionist

Lazzy's escape had us baffled for a while. We came up with explanations like, "He must've squeezed out between the gate frame and the gate," or "He slipped out before Godfrey secured the gate during his feeding the night before." But all these theories seemed highly unlikely. The space that one could force between the gate and its frame was far too narrow to allow him to fit through. And there was no chance that he could sneak past Godfrey without him noticing. Godfrey was always incredibly careful when opening the enclosure during feeding. The mystery drove us nearly mad.

A few days later, we arrived at the enclosure to find Lazzy waiting for us on the sandbank outside his release pen. As usual, he was absolutely thrilled to see us, running to each of us in turn to say hello. I walked over to his enclosure to find the gate locked. The additional wires we had used to fasten the gate so as to allow no movement or gap between the gate and frame, were exactly as we had left them. I again inspected the boundaries of the enclosure and the ground for where he may have dug his way out, as well as the corners where the fence connected to the wooden poles. Everything was tight and secure.

Lazzy followed me as I did this, and I had hoped that he would drop me a clue, but there was none. "Lazzy my boy, where are you getting out? You are quite the little escape artist, aren't you? Our little Houdini!"

We walked Lazarus down to the river for the usual day of activities. The kids asked if they could float down the river with the current, and so Brendan took them up to the camp, a high point from where they could start. He got in the water with them to keep an eye on them. Spencer and Rebecca screamed with laughter as the currents took control of their movements and they floated along the top of the water. Lazzy seemed alarmed by their shrill screams. He raised his head, nose in the air as if to discern whether they were calling for help. He responded with a chirp.

As they came into sight, he darted off after them and joined them in their fun. He swam circles around them. He darted under the water, each time popping up on the opposite side of them. It was remarkable how long he could hold his breath and how comfortably he moved in the water. They were delighted to have him as company.

It was a beautiful day that we hoped would never end. We ate our lunch under the trees while Lazzy foraged in the river.

"I think the day out on his own did him good," I remarked. "He explored a wider section of his environment and understands now how to get back to his enclosure, in case he needs our support."

"Yes, it gave him the opportunity to learn without our influence, completely on his own, making up his own mind. That's good," agreed Brendan.

"Looks like we may go off-plan here," I said.

We had a marked-out period that we had believed would be necessary to get the otter ready for the wild before his release, but he was proving himself ready long before that. "It looks like Lazzy has a plan of his own."

Lazarus was not only learning how to look after himself but also how to be by himself. He was becoming more independent. Although he still very much enjoyed our company, I noticed he was moving further and further away from us during these times at the river. Whereas before he wouldn't have dared to leave our side, he was now wandering around on his own and exploring sections along the river unaccompanied. Independence was the final requirement we had hoped for in the process that would make Lazzy's release a success. He was slowly letting us know that he was ready and that it was time for us to let go. But right now, we would put the release off for another day when we would be able to camp out for the night and observe him during his first night in the wild.

Chapter 17

The Mystery Solved

We walked back up the embankment to where the enclosure stood. Lazarus followed and, as if programmed, ran and jumped straight inside to lie down in his favourite spot on the porch of his wooden house. It was getting late; the sun was low, as if resting briefly on the surface of the water before disappearing for the night. Brendan fastened the gate of the enclosure. We were about to leave when Lazzy ran to the side of the enclosure, giving us that look of bewilderment, as if to say, "That's it, you're leaving me here?"

Then he climbed up the side of his wire mesh cage and within minutes he was out and standing next to us again. We both stood dumbfounded for a minute or so, then laughed at our ignorance. He had undoubtedly outsmarted us. In all this time, none of us had thought to check the roof of the enclosure! In the corner of the roof, almost directly above the gate, was a perfectly round hole exactly big enough for an otter to fit through.

When we built the enclosure, we used thick welded mesh for the sides; we specifically picked an indestructible material to construct it from. But for the roof, we used a thinner mesh panel, which we had available from an old enclosure for the owls that was no longer in use. I remember saying to Brendan, "I'm sure this will do just fine. It should be strong enough for what we need. It's not like he would try and break through the roof." The irony of those words echoed in my head.

Brendan unpacked tools and materials from the Land Rover to patch up the hole, at least temporarily until it was time to let him out. We had planned to set up a camera to monitor Lazzy's movements and camera traps that would send footage on email to keep an eye on him when we were off the farm, before we would leave him to fend for himself. I distracted Lazarus on the opposite side of the enclosure while Brendan set to work. When the job was finished, we stood back to admire his craftsmanship.

"He's not getting through that," he said.

"That's for sure," I agreed.

Lazzy climbed up to take a closer look for himself. When he realized that his escape hole had been covered up, he moved along the side of the fence, checking other sections of the roof, prodding and feeling over parts of it. His hands moved fast like a disc jockey on a mixer, testing the robustness of the entire roof area.

"Well, I'll be damned!" I exclaimed.

Before long, Lazzy had managed to find another weak spot. From a minuscule piece of loose wire that broke away from the interlinked mesh, he set to work undoing the criss-cross pattern of the wire mesh roof. He used his tiny human-like fingers to undo the wirework, untangling it little by little with ease and meticulous perfection. I stood stupefied, gawking at what was unfolding in front of our very eyes. Lazarus demonstrated cognitive reasoning abilities far beyond anything I had ever observed in, or thought possible for, an animal.

He must have used the time he had inside his enclosure to inspect and scrutinise every corner of the structure that kept him trapped. With willpower and determination, he formulated a clear plan of escape. But how did he know to unravel the intricate pattern of wirework? Over and under he twisted the wire, unwinding it to make the hole. To identify a pattern demonstrates an exceptionally high level of intelligence. He also showed an ability to think with clear logic and had even used spatial reasoning in his master plan. The hole he made was the perfect fit for him to slip through, and he had used the hole to leave the enclosure whenever he pleased.

I was exhilarated by this proof of animal intelligence, especially in an otter. This proved the strong correlation between animal and human behaviour, judgement, reasoning, and intellect - similarities far greater than most would care to admit. If we could demonstrate the affinity between people and the animal kingdom, maybe more of us would be inclined to protect those we once believed to be nothing more than unfeeling beasts reacting on instinct alone as the driving force that guides their behaviour. In the words of Charles Darwin (1838), "It is hard to say what is instinct in animals and what is reason, in precisely the same way it is impossible to say what is habitual in men and what reasonable...as man has hereditary tendencies, therefore man's mind is not so different from that of brutes."

We made the decision there and then to open the enclosure gate and to permanently leave it open from now on. Lazzy had made the decision of the timing of his release for us.

That night marked the last time that he would live confined. We could not deny him his freedom any longer. He had passed every single test we had given him with flying colours. He had proven to us over and over again that he was smart enough to adapt to the wild. He approached his tasks with such unfaltering energy and determination that we were able to say with complete confidence that he would make it out there on his own.

"My clever little boy! You are finally ready to live your life wild and free like you were supposed to."

Lazzy relaxes with Brendan (left) and Godfrey (right) on the riverbank.

Lazzy walks with a haughty stride with his fish to go and eat it in a quiet spot along the river.

Lazzy is bushed after an eventful day in the river.

Lazzy confidently swims and plays with Brendan in the deep section of the river.

Chapter 18

Return to the Wild

That moment when we had decided to allow Lazzy to go free was one of the best moments of my life. When we opened the gate to his cage for evermore and allowed him his own free will, my heart swelled and every limb in my body had a feeling of lightness in it, as if I was floating through clouds of merriment. It was as if a small part of the universe had been set right. In my heart I knew that he was going to be okay - more than that, he was going to be happy. He finally had the opportunity to live his life the way nature had intended it before an unfortunate incident had set his life off-course. The expected feelings of sadness at letting go were completely absent, and I felt content in the knowledge that Lazzy was where he was meant to be. He had been returned to the wild.

It was not goodbye, of course. Not yet, anyway. It simply meant that our control over his movements had fallen away, and when and where we saw him was completely up to him from now onwards. At that point, in one of the final parts of our adventure with Lazzy, it was impossible to deny the innate dangers that are contained within freedom. We again had to confront our fears of the uncertainties of the otter's future. In any natural environment, like the one he was in, he would have to navigate his way around predators and he would have threats to circumvent. We had to trust that Lazarus was ready to take on these challenges that come with survival in the wilderness, and we had to have faith in our teachings and the skills he had learned during this time we had spent with him, allowing him to prepare for the life that awaited him.

If there was one thing we knew for sure, now more than ever, it was that Lazarus could master new skills in a flash. He learned quickly. His curiosity will continue to feed his inquisitive mind with information about the environment he finds himself in. After witnessing his problem-solving abilities that led to his escape, I knew that he would be able to think on his feet. Lazzy is only but a small otter, but he is lion-hearted. He is brave and determined, two characteristics that will serve him well in his new life.

It was about three days after we had made the decision to permanently leave the gate of Lazzy's enclosure open that Godfrey came to me with a video he had taken the day before. "I want to show you something," he said. "You won't believe this."

The video was of a snake hanging from the tree next to Lazzy's enclosure. The footage was taken with a poor-quality camera, but the imagery was good enough to identify a black mamba before it slithered off and disappeared into the bush. It was unmistakable. There, only metres from where Lazzy lived, was one of the most feared snakes in Africa.

The black mamba is a highly venomous snake that commonly grows to 3 m long - the second longest venomous snake in the world. It is both fast and aggressive. This mamba gets its name from the ink-blackness of the inside of its mouth and not the colour of its skin, which is more brownish or silvery-grey. If bitten by one, you would most likely keel over in less than an hour from the time the venom enters your bloodstream. And without treatment, you would most likely meet your end that same day. I shuddered at the thought of it slithering into Lazzy's enclosure to crawl up in the shade of his wooden house.

Then the irony struck me. All that time, when we thought that Lazzy was safe and protected because he was in captivity, our thoughts were not entirely true and were clearly an illusion. In captivity, Lazarus had been trapped. If the snake had slithered its way into his enclosure while Lazzy was still in it, he would have had no prospect of escaping the danger of an aggressive and dangerous snake like a mamba. The otter was much better off in the wild, where he could move and behave naturally.

Weeks after Lazzy's release, he would still meet us at the same spot by the river. He kept to the territorial area of his release enclosure. For weeks we continued to go every day to check up on him and to make sure that he was doing okay. At first, we still took him fish and food to eat, but after a while realised that he no longer needed it and the fish was simply going to waste. He showed no interest in it. He was the picture of health and obviously enjoyed all the delectable nourishments the river provided.

He was always happy to see us. He would come over to greet us, and you could swear that there was a smile on his face whenever he saw us. Lazzy has an amiable nature and this he could transfer with a simple look. It was impossible to have a bad day around Lazarus; he would always lighten the mood. If he had been a person, he would be the sociable and fun-loving kind. The life of the party. He would seek out entertainment and be energised by social interactions, loving most of all the attention on himself.

It was amazing how many genuine human characteristics one could ascribe to Lazzy. He would be the kind of person who is open to new experiences, curious about the world around him, and who thinks outside the box. A confident person who naturally draws people to him. He would also be a calm and collected person who rarely concerns himself over frivolous things. He would be both athletic and brainy. Above all, he would be kind, generous, and caring. He would be the kind of person anyone would like to have as a friend, and we considered ourselves lucky to have him in our lives.

Lazarus still enjoyed spending time with us, even though he had the freedom to move around as he pleased. He would swim with Brendan, run around, play with us, and stay within the area where he could see us for a while, as if nothing had changed. Then, when he had spent enough time there, he would slowly start wandering further along the river, through the vegetation along the banks, until he would eventually pass out of sight. We would watch as he explored, picking up molluscs and pieces of crabs and shells, bringing them to his mouth to taste them and then dropping the shells back in the water, as he made his way along the shallows.

The next day, he would repeat the same practice and...the day after... and the day after that. Each day, we would get a short time with him, a quick hello, before he continued with his day's activities, shifting his focus to otter things.

Where Is the Fish?

By Brendan Murray

Early on a Wednesday morning at around 6:00, only 12 days after Lazzy's official release, I drove to the release farm to go spend the day fishing with him. It was a pleasant drive through the countryside, with plenty of vegetable and cotton farms in the west and game farms to the east. This road had almost no traffic except for the occasional tractor that drove less than 20 km per hour. As pleasant as the hour-and-twenty-minutes it took each day to make the trip was, every one of those journeys was filled with a bit of anxiety. Will I be able to find him?

On this day, he was waiting for me at the top of the pathway that leads down to the river. He was soaking wet, which meant that he had been in the water when he heard the Land Rover approaching - which in his mind was as though Uber Eats had arrived to deliver a fresh load of fish for only him to enjoy. He had left the river specifically to meet me. Lazzy could catch his own fish by now, but that didn't mean that he didn't appreciate a free meal. But I had no fish with me on that day, only fishing tackle. My idea was to go and catch a barbel (catfish) for the little monster's breakfast.

Lazarus had learnt very quickly where the fish was kept. When the Landy came to a stop, he would climb in the back to help, in his own way, to offload the fish. That day being no different, he climbed in and when he couldn't find any fish, he decided to crawl in under the back passenger seat. I tried to coerce him out by making as if I was walking to the river, but he was having so much fun inspecting the Land Rover that he paid me no attention. Alas, he was not at all interested in going to the river and must have been convinced that I was hiding the fish somewhere.

While I was getting the bait ready for fishing, I received a call about a couple of young marsh owls that had been sold to an informal muthi (traditional medicine) market just outside Potchefstroom. Rescuing wildlife from these markets is always an urgent issue, so I had to leave immediately. I pleaded with Lazzy to vacate the vehicle and promised that I would catch up with him a little later in the day. The location where I had to rescue the marsh owls was around 200 km away.

I felt so guilty for leaving so soon after my arrival, and my failed plan of catching him a fish, that I thought it would be best to stop at a fish market on the way back. I rescued the owlets and was back at the river in just under five hours. I ended up paying R280 for a rather small mackerel, but to return with a gift for Lazzy was well worth it. And he was rather pleased with his fish.

Chapter 19

The First Rains

The rains came later than usual that spring. It had been a hot and dry season, but when the clouds finally decided to burst open, the sky turned fiercely dark and the rain came bucketing down. I woke to the sound of a ferocious crack of lightning followed by the rumbling of thunder. I sat up in bed, my heart fluttering in my chest. My thoughts went straight to Lazarus. This would be the first thunderstorm that he would experience on his own out in the wild. My usual love of electric skies and wet weather turned to an ominous atmosphere of fear, uncertainty, and forsakenness.

Brendan turned in bed to face me. "That's quite a storm," he whispered under his breath.

"I'm worried about him," I said.

I did not have to explain. Brendan knew that I meant Lazzy and he, too, felt uneasy knowing that the little otter had to weather the storm all on his own, without any prior knowledge of what to expect of his new environment during heavy rainfalls. Will he know to find cover? Will he get to higher ground when the river's water level rises? Will he understand the changes in the river - the strong flowing force of the water and rapid currents? These were all thoughts that haunted me.

"He will be fine," Brendan reassured me, "He'll figure things out. We'll leave at first light to go and check on him."

I lay awake for a good few hours listening to the crashing sounds of thunder and lightning, pondering over Lazzy's first exposure to the perpetually frightening and wholly unexpected storm. My mind travelled back to that day when he got swept away in the river and how he cried out in panic, imploring us to protect him from an uncertain fate. His helplessness during that ordeal had unsettled me, and left me feeling uncertain of his ability to adapt to such a dangerous environment and our high, maybe even unrealistic, expectations of him to develop the necessary survival skills. For many days after that incident, it played on my mind.

But then I remembered how quickly he shook off that bad experience and used it as a learning opportunity to understand the river. He learned respect for the fast-flowing body of water and to appreciate its power and intensity. I reminded myself of the rapid progress he had made over a very short time and how quickly he had grasped new concepts. I reassured myself that this experience will be no different and that he would instinctively know what to do.

The next morning we arrived at our normal spot, but Lazarus was nowhere to be seen. My chest tightened and a horrible feeling of hopelessness came over me. The river and landscape had changed significantly because of the storm. The water was higher than usual. The island where we used to play with Lazzy, where he would roll around in the sand and bake in the sun and where he would enjoy his usual meal, was no longer visible. The sandbank was flooded, completely covered in water. It was as if the setting I remembered in my mind's eye was never there, as though we had imagined the whole scene. There was a strangeness to this place which we carried such deep nostalgic memories of. Some of the grass that grew near the river's edge had been flattened by the force of the water, as if to bow down to its cruelty. What was worse was that Lazzy was completely absent from the entire scene.

We started calling out to him, desperate to find him safe and sound. All along the river, the clay soil was patterned with many deeply tramped, defined animal footprints left behind in the slush. Along one section it seemed as if a hippo had slipped on the muddy slope in a long struggle to exit the water. It looked like a scene of panic. Hooves and paws left traces that told a story about the night before, but none of these tracks were otter prints. There was no evidence of Lazzy at all, no clues left behind to ease our grave concern.

"Lazzeey...Lazzy...Lazzeey!" we constantly called. We persevered in our search for what felt like hours, until finally there was an answer back. A squeak could be heard about 50 m further upriver. The second squeak confirmed it—our precious boy had heard our cries.

The sky was crystal blue. The surroundings had an appearance of luminous clarity. You could see all the way into the wild blue yonder. It was only when I heard Lazzy that I realized how beautiful it all was. The whole ecosystem was buzzing with new life. We made our way in the general direction of where we had heard his reply. I was overjoyed with relief. Tears welled up in my eyes, as if all the emotion caused by my fear and uncertainty needed to leave my body somehow. With every call after that, Lazzy answered back, as if in echo. I smiled through my tears as we made our way over to him.

On the side of the riverbank ahead, a curious head peaked out of a den. He extended his neck from the hole and, without leaving the safety of his burrow just yet, took a stealthy look to see if what he had thought he had heard was in fact true, that we were really there to check on him. The time that passed during the storm must have been exaggerated in his mind. Bad experiences always seem longer than what they are, as though there will be no end to it. He seemed relieved when he caught sight of us. He left the den and came over to where we were. Through squeals and murmured noises, he audibly expressed his excitement to see us.

It was obvious that he must have been frightened. Without explanation or reason, he had suddenly found himself in a world of unfamiliar, menacing events. There were booming, thunderous noises all around him, noises he had never heard out there in the wild before. Water poured down unexpectedly from the sky above him and it must have seemed that there was no escape from its vicious spate. The environment he had learned to manoeuvre in so well had become alien to him again. It was incomparable to anything he had previously encountered in his entire life. Some would feel that in captivity he was protected from these natural elements, while I believe that he had instead been deprived.

Despite this, he braved the storm and got himself to safety. Lazzy proved once more that he is a resourceful fellow, capable of quick thinking and with an ability to acclimate. This may have been his first storm, but it will certainly not be his last. In his life ahead, he will need to weather many more storms. He will have challenges to live through, dangers to survive, and elements to withstand. Each new experience he encounters prepares him for the next, giving him the courage and confidence to get through it and to triumph over the savage wilderness. The moments of darkness are the seeds of his transformation. Some skills can only be gained when brief suffering is not only faced but embraced. As time passes, he will become better equipped to survive and combat the next obstacle that comes his way. With this increased confidence also comes a growing need for autonomy.

In the weeks to come, Lazarus would remind us of his new-found independence as a wild-living otter. He had become more and more self-sufficient as time went by, and he had come to rely on himself more. This meant that he was not only physically free but moving toward becoming entirely free from his previous captive life. He had freed his mind. Unfettered from his past human dependence, he became self-standing. He reminded me of a teenager ready to launch into adulthood, who while respectfully acknowledging his parents would rebel against any influence or control over his decisions and push towards living his own liberated, wilful life.

We encouraged Lazzy's independence and made the decision to visit less frequently, stretching the periods in between longer and longer to allow him to make a full transition into the wild. This was a hard decision to make, but it was because of our deep love for Lazzy that we were determined to do what was best for him. We had to break all ties Lazarus still had to the human world. We would observe Lazarus from a distance, and analyze his movements and behaviour to determine whether he had adjusted as well as we had hoped.

Godfrey kept an eye on him for us on the days that we were not there, sending us updates and reports on where he had spotted him. On one occasion, he sent us a video of a female otter that had entered Lazzy's territory, and we were all overly excited. We had high hopes that Lazarus had attracted a female and found himself a mate. If he had indeed found a mate, it would mean that the little guy would have joined the natural cycle of life as it was intended, and his legacy would continue with a future generation of otters. In that, his life would fulfil its purpose and would contribute to the survival of the species.

Chapter 20

The End Is Also the Beginning

"Don't cry because it's over, smile because it happened." - *Dr. Seuss*

It was a delightful day to be out in nature. The birds were chirping in soft melody, like a ceremonial bushveld song. The earth was buzzing with life. Creatures all around us were busily at work. A determined dung beetle rolled a large ball of dung twice his own size along the dirt road, using his back legs to push and roll it in the direction he wanted it, carefully readjusting his aim to keep control of the smooth, round bundle of animal excrement. A weaver bird flew back and forth, tirelessly fetching and carrying blades of grass to build a new nest.

On the opposite side of the river, in the tall savanna grass, a giraffe stood with her legs apart for a calf to plummet from nigh on 2 m high to the ground, front feet and neck stretched out forward, as it emerged into the world. Shortly after birth, the calf struggled to its feet to take its first few steps on the harsh and unstable earth. There would be little time to waste. Soon this little giraffe would have to run to keep up with its mum. Mother Nature keeps a clock of her own, on which all survival depends. It progresses at an expeditious pace, yet never seems to be rushed. Everything seems to be calm and restful, while growth transpires ceaselessly and smoothly like an arrow from a bow.

Like the river, the environment around us constantly moves and changes. Lazarus had changed, too, and was no longer the same otter we met those many months ago. Mother Nature had welcomed him home, like she does with all of her own, and taught him the ways of the wild. We had watched him transform right in front of our very eyes. He spontaneously underwent many changes because he understood what was required of him to ensure his own survival in the, albeit pleasing, unsympathetic wilderness. Watching him adapt to his surroundings made me realize (again) how much better animals are equipped compared to humans.

We humans have believed for many years that we are the highest-ranking species, bragging about our superior intelligence, yet if you had to measure our instinctive survival skills and compare them to those of animals, you'd find them to be no match. What's more, where animals contribute to their environment, we generally bring about destruction. We change our environment to suit us, but animals change, grow, and develop to fit into their environment instead. The entire basis of evolution is based on this development. By changing our environment, often through damaging behaviour, we set off a whole chain of events that cause catastrophic consequences. If we could change or adapt ourselves instead, we would only become a better and stronger species.

We sat day after day in the river on a pontoon boat made from two large hollow drums attached to a wooden platform, slowly drifting along and watching, searching and hoping to spot Lazarus. Some days we were lucky and Lazzy would be playing around, but sometimes several days would pass without us seeing him at all. Frequently we would spot him on the embankment or in the river foliage where he would perk his head up, but only momentarily before carrying on as if we were not there, completely disinterested in our presence. We kept watch, often through binoculars, even though we knew that it could be hours of waiting and observing without any trace of Lazarus at all.

He had become a part of the wild and wondrous world and lived by its natural order. It had become more for our personal reasons, for our own peace of mind and our curiosity, that we continued to go back to where Lazarus was. He had stopped needing us. We had reached the finish line of his release process and our role in his journey was over. For Lazzy, it was merely the beginning of a new life in the wild. As for us, concluding such a meaningful assignment stirred up a keen interest in projects aimed at protecting and conserving otter species.

One day, Rebecca was playing in a shallow part of the river. She sat on a small section of island with her legs tucked in underneath her, up to her waist in slow-flowing water. I could see that she was deep in thought. She sat entranced by the elegant movements of a bright red dragonfly dancing on the surface of the river. It looked like a fairy with its shimmering, rainbow-coloured wings. She was reminiscing about the friendship she had shared with an otter who she may never see again. She sat motionless and lost in her thoughts. How quickly things had changed. How much it must be for a little mind to process ...

Then, out of nowhere, Lazarus came swimming right up to her.

"Lazzy!" she cried in astonishment.

The otter gently nudged Rebecca with his nose and, frolicking around her, he nibbled on her hands. He swam in circles around her, spinning and twisting his body in the water before hopping onto her lap. Then he quietly sat next to her for a while, his neck stretched out as if to see what she had been staring at those few minutes before he came up to her. They had a moment out there, the two of them, in which they said their farewells.

After a while, he quietly slipped into the water and drifted along the river until he vanished into the thick green vegetation along the water's edge. She would later tell me that she believed he could hear her thoughts.

"He must've known how much I missed him and that I was wondering where he was," she professed.

I smiled at her, pleased with her contentment. It is a memory that will stay with her for all her life.

We walked back up to where Lazzy's enclosure stood empty and purposeless. It suddenly seemed inappropriate and out of place in this setting, and we paused for a minute to discuss our plans to take it down. Across from the enclosure, on the opposite side of the pathway, was a beautiful large hamerkop nest. A hamerkop (the name translated directly from Afrikaans means "hammer head") is one of my favourite birds for the reason I could only describe as an intrinsic fascination. The hamerkop (*Scopus umbretta*) is classified in a genus of his own, a unique bird indeed.

They build nests purely for the enjoyment of it, an activity which both genders partake in; they build several nests a year whether they are breeding or not. Hammerkop birds are, the way I see it, the architects and artists of the animal kingdom. Their nests are enormous, made from thousands of sticks and bundles of grass held together by mud cement, constructed strong enough to hold the weight of an adult human. They seem to prefer a room with a view, and nests are usually found near the water's edge. They start by building the indestructible stick-and-mud foundation platform for the nest, then they construct strong steady walls with an arched roof.

The domed entrance, plastered with mud, leads into a tunnel that is linked to the main boudoir - a room which comfortably accommodates the parents and their offspring. Improvements to the home are often made, even after the pair has moved in and eggs been laid. Colourful decorations adorn the outside of the nest. For them, it is about more than just creating a functional nest; instead, the pair use the nest building process as an opportunity to bond with each other through the expression of their creativity. And for other birds such as owls, these nests are top realty. Fortunately for them, hamerkops are compulsive nest builders and seem to do this for a hobby, so there are often vacant ones readily available to move into.

We had first noticed the hamerkop nest on the water's edge when we were deciding on a spot to build Lazarus's enclosure. It was a few metres further along the embankment from the place we had picked for the release pen. We were extra cautious and mindful to have minimal impact on the environment and area where we would erect the structure, and when we spotted the nest we made sure that we were far enough from it not to cause any disturbance to the potentially nesting birds.

Jonas Chirwa, a Malawian man who helped us build the enclosure, told me a story about a hamerkop's nest while we were busily at work erecting the structure that would become Lazzy's temporary home. "In my culture it is believed that a person who breaks down a hamerkop's nest will be cursed and become deranged," he said.

I listened intently as he conveyed the African folklore he grew up with. I loved this story for its perfect metaphor of my own belief of what may happen to the human race if we continue on the path of destruction.

I cannot help but believe that our sanity is linked to our relationship with nature, whether we care to admit it or not. I know, for one, that mine is. There is a reason why flowers make us smile, why a potted plant brings life to a room - even a goldfish has the ability to make us feel less lonely in the world. This innate attraction to nature was first explained by a German psychologist named Erich Fromm, who used the term "biophilia" to elaborate on the human-nature relationship. Edward O. Wilson later popularised the term in a 1984 book called *Biophilia*. In it he explained that it is human instinct to be drawn to, be connected to, and have a need to be affiliated with other forms of living things, such as animals and plants.

Even though modern life has pushed us further and further away from our inherent connection to nature - fter all, we are, as we come to realize more every day, not that far removed from animals - a part of our brain still remembers our intrinsic wild side. Just like Lazarus remembered, through spending time in his natural environment, how to be a wild otter, we too have the ability to discover a more positive side of ourselves, given the chance to reconnect ourselves again with the living world. It is through this connection that our spirit experiences absolute freedom. Nature is where we find our equilibrium. It is where the self-constructed walls of our ego melt away and we become part of something bigger than ourselves; we become a part of the universe. In this, we become whole.

Connecting to your inner wild side does not mean that you have to live like a social outcast and move to a deserted cabin in the dense and lonely woods - it simply means taking more time to appreciate nature in our immediate surroundings, and to add to it by planting a tree or even a little shrub wherever we can. The saying, "Stop to smell the roses," comes to mind. We should all make time in our busy day to walk outside, kick off our shoes, and stand barefoot on the earth while meticulously taking in everything around us, to remind us that despite how the world has changed, we are still at heart rooted in nature. A habit as small as this is very often the start of something much larger - an appreciation, in essence, for all that is living.

Thirteen species of otters, all of which are under threat, inhabit this planet, each facing a decline in their population. In working with Lazarus, I realized that if Brendan and I really want to make a difference in conservation, we would need to do far more than simply save one individual otter from a life spent in captivity. Or even rescue, rehabilitate, and release several hundreds of owls every year. In the bigger scheme of things, we are doing nothing more than fighting a losing battle. Every day we wake up confronted by the same concerns about wildlife persecution because people fail to understand the true nature of these creatures. Owls are, still today, associated with witchcraft or perceived as a messenger from some or other "dark force." Every day we receive calls from people asking us to remove and relocate owls from urban areas to prevent their killing.

Once, Brendan was asked to remove an entire owl family nesting on school grounds. He did so reluctantly, and not before trying his utmost to convince the principal to let them stay, explaining the benefits of having the owls around. He also offered to educate the children on owls and their importance in the ecosystem. But the headmaster was not convinced, nor were the teachers who had joined the conversation.

"You don't understand the kids of today," he blurted out, "They cannot be reasoned with."

The three teachers nodded their heads in agreement. "I had to stop one from using the baby owl they had found sitting under a tree as a soccer ball," one of the teachers explained. "I fear that if you don't take them all, they will be killed."

This was a worrying scenario; not even the educators themselves felt that they had any sway over the perceptions of these children and their intolerance of wild animals.

If we are to protect owls and other wildlife, we need to aim to conserve the entire species rather than try to rescue and rehabilitate a few individual ones. Wildlife rehabilitation, although important work, has its limitations. It treats the symptoms of a world that is slowly losing touch with its natural elements, but it is not dealing with the underlying cause of the "disease" that is driving wildlife to the brink of extinction. My interest over the past years has grown significantly towards the protection of vulnerable wildlife, habitat preservation, restoration, and management. But I have also realised that the only way to succeed in this is to find a way to achieve global participation.

In principle, this would mean diminishing the divide between humans and nature - bringing people closer to the natural world. How we can accomplish this, I am not entirely sure. Many before us have tried and failed. Whenever we can, Brendan and I gather information and compile research on human-animal conflict as well as the most severe threats to natural habitat that will help us to formulate a plan. We dream about one day taking some time off from our busy rehabilitation work at the Owl Sanctuary to sail around the world in a yacht. We would seek out people from other countries who might help us in our quest to protect what is dear to us. We would meet with people from all walks of life to learn and gain knowledge, which we could apply to make a valuable contribution to the conservation of our precious biodiversity. We also want to spend time on different coastlines studying otters, an animal that has captured our imagination unlike any other and has earned a special place in our hearts.

Whenever I feel downhearted, I take a long slow walk through the Sanctuary, seeking out owls roosting in large shady trees that have been released after their rehabilitation from injury or illness, and through the process have been given a new lease on life. To lose confidence in oneself is common in our line of work, and I often find myself grabbing on to whatever bit of encouragement I can find. Sometimes it feels like I am running a race, stopping at brief intervals to catch my breath, hunched over and gulping for air, gathering just enough strength to propel me forward to continue on with the next part of it. I get overwhelmed when it seems as though there is no end in sight.

On these walks, I take a long pause at each of the owls, as if to have a silent conversation with each one and remind myself that Brendan and I have had an impact on their lives. We have helped to change the course of their life, even if just in a small way. And because of that, my life has meaning.

If I had to tell you exactly how many owls there are in the Sanctuary, I would have to tell a lie. They are all over the place. What I can say with complete surety is that I am convinced that it is the highest population of free-living owls in the world. The Sanctuary provides a safe environment for recovering owls where they can get used to the wild, before they move off to find a new territory. Some of these rescued owls who struggle to readapt remain in the Sanctuary for longer, sometimes permanent, as feeding platforms located in accessible areas all over the farm provides an easy meal. Farms surrounding the Sanctuary have reported sightings of new breeding pairs. A species that they have not seen for years is taking up residence in the area.

Working with animals has taught me to push my personal boundaries. I know that there is always the possibility of failing at what we set out to accomplish. So many things could have gone wrong in our plan to set Lazarus free. Many naysayers said it would be impossible for an animal to survive after living so long in captivity, but that should not discourage us from trying. There is victory in the trying alone. What we have learned through this entire process is invaluable.

With a stroke of luck, Lazzy's release turned out exactly the way we had hoped.

Our relationship with the otter progressed naturally, with his self-sufficiency growing stronger with every passing day. I no longer feared that he was too tame or had imprinted on humans. He answered the call of the wild, a cry from somewhere deep within him that could be only momentarily silenced. This voice would not be stifled. Lazarus is unconfined, happy, and healthy. His inquisitive mind can finally be stimulated by the natural wonders around him. He lives each day in the here and now, cheerfully, without any regret or dismay about the past. He stepped into his new life courageously embracing his fears, overcoming obstacles and in doing so gained the ultimate reward - freedom.

The thing I've found most inspirational and rewarding in my work with wildlife is experiencing their capacity to live in the present. They start each new day with the same will and drive to continue, to exist. Animals cannot express their gratitude like humans do through language and the spoken word. They do something far greater than that. Lazzy expressed his gratitude through living his best life. We have all helped people in our lives who have disappointed us in one way or another, often by falling back into their all-too-familiar bad habits. How I wish we possessed animals' spirit and will to survive.

I will always be grateful to Lazarus for the impression he made on our lives. He left deep footprints on our hearts. He changed something within us forever. Of course, we will have many more experiences and encounters with animals that will enrich our lives, but none will be quite like Lazzy.

We never said goodbye to him, only farewell until we meet again. There is always the possibility, on some sunny day by the river, of a chance encounter where we could meet like old friends and remember the precious times we had together. Years from now we will still return to our favourite meeting spot in the hope of getting a glimpse of him. Maybe we will find him there alone, or maybe he will have a family. How the story of this otter's life unfolds from here on out is left entirely up to fate and Nature's spontaneous timeline.

An underwater photo of a water-confident Lazzy.

Lazzy visits Rebecca
in the river